the POST-APOCALYPTIC primer

K. SCOTT BRADBURY

Cover photo by K. Scott Bradbury

Disclaimer: This book is presented for entertainment and informational purposes only. The information provided in this book is designed to provide helpful information on the subjects discussed. No warranties or guarantees are expressed or implied by the author's choice to include any of the content in this volume. Neither the publisher nor the author shall be liable for any physical, psychological, emotional, financial, or commercial damages, including, but not limited to, special, incidental, consequential or other damages. The reader is encouraged to seek professional advice before taking action and to comply with all local and federal laws. The reader accepts responsibility for their own choices, actions, and results. Readers should be aware that the websites listed in this book may change.

Copyright © 2010 K. Scott Bradbury
All rights reserved.

Printed by CreateSpace, Charleston, SC

ISBN: 1453791485
ISBN-13: 9781453791486
LCCN: 2010917694

Contents

Foreward   v

Introduction   ix

Chapter 1   Identifying Your Apocalypse   1
    Global Warming/Ice Age   2
    Nuclear War   9
    Alien Invasion   12
    Robot Holocaust   15
    Seismic Catastrophe   19
    Meteors/Asteroids/Comets   24
    Disease   27
    Zombies   29
    Religious End Times   31
    Apocalypse Hybridization Matrix (HAM)   34

Chapter 2   What To Expect   37
    General Disaster Conditions   37
    Specific Disaster Conditions   39

Chapter 3   Stages Of Disorder   43
    Instant Apocalypse   43
    Apocalypse: Coming Soon!   45
    The Slow-Burn Apocalypse   47

Chapter 4   Assessing Your Existing Survival Skills   51
    Location, Location, Location   51
    Your Vocation   53

Your Hobbies	54
Post-Apocalyptic Survival and Success Assessment (PASSA)	55

Chapter 5 Civilization After The Fall Of Civilization — 73
- Social Pockets Of The Post-Apocalypse — 74
- Careers Of The Post-Apocalypse — 82
- Politics Of The Post-Apocalypse — 89

Chapter 6 Fight Or Die — 93
- Identifying Threats — 93
- Tools Of The Trade — 96

Chapter 7 The Apocalypse Is Mobile — 105
- The Need For Mobility — 105
- Land Travel — 106
- Water Travel — 107
- Air Travel — 109

Chapter 8 Eat, Drink, And Be Wary — 113
- Water, Water, Everywhere? — 113
- What's For Dinner — 115
- Talking About The Taboo — 117

Chapter 9 Survivor, Heal Thyself — 119
- Where Did All The Doctors Go? — 120
- An Ounce Of Prevention — 121
- That Healing Touch — 122

Chapter 10 Knowledge Is Power — 125
- Recommended Reading — 126
- Internet Resources — 134

Foreword

There are big lessons we should have learned from the three biggest events in recent American history- 9/11, hurricane Katrina, and the Gulf oil spill. First came 9/11. A group of religious fanatics attempted to bring down America in a single day. They successfully attacked and destroyed a literal and symbolic pillar of the American economy, the World Trade Center. They attacked and partially destroyed our military's heart, the Pentagon. Had it not been for the bravery of a few civilians, the terrorists might have also succeeded in attacking the Capitol building or the White House. And they pulled it off right under the nose of the largest and most sophisticated intelligence community on the planet.

More lessons arrived in New Orleans in the form of Hurricane Katrina. A tragedy unfolded before us on TV as we watched the citizens of New Orleans drown because they relied on the local, state, and Federal government to keep them safe from danger and rescue them if they needed it. How many died because they were assured by authorities they were safe where they were or died waiting for government transportation that never came or died waiting for military rescuers that were not dispatched in time or died in refugee facilities that were ruled by chaos and anarchy? America's government, one of the richest on Earth, with over 13 million employees could not rescue a single city in peril.

Most recently, the Gulf oil spill demonstrated once more that while the U.S. possesses some of the most formidable economic, intellectual, civil, and military resources on Earth, its government is incapable of marshalling those powers to respond to an emergency in a timely manner. Worse yet, governmental bureaucracy may make the situation worse by putting up obstacles that prevent civilian and foreign assistance when it is most needed.

At first glance, this may sound like some anti-government diatribe but that is not the intent here. The intent is to illustrate that in spite of the immense power and scope of governments they are, in the end, quite fallible. Governments cannot be counted on to detect every threat. Governments can fail to act due to political and bureaucratic overlap. Government oversight can fail to safeguard the environment. Governments do not always have the political authority or will to marshal all the resources at their disposal. The big lesson these events should impart to you is that the only one that you can really rely on to save you from disaster and anarchy is you.

You are not a paranoid crackpot. No one mocks you for having a rainy day fund or buying health insurance or wearing your seatbelt. You're just taking reasonable precautions against possible or probable events. But if you prepare for catastrophe, people give you sideways looks that imply you're not quite right in the head. And yet being ready for a calamity is just another way you are taking precautions to protect you and your loved ones. How does caring about the safety of your family make you a crackpot? If anything, in light of all the historical evidence, it's highly irrational to *not* take precautions against natural and man-made cataclysms that could leave the environment and/or society in shambles.

You're not a crackpot because we *do* face natural and man-made threats to our civilization and your governments *cannot* be relied on to protect you from said threats. Those are facts, not paranoid conspiracies or nutty theories, and those facts exist for everyone regardless of your political or religious leanings (or lack thereof). It is sincerely hoped that the events and conditions described in this book never come to be. But if they do, it

K. Scott Bradbury

is better to have knowledge about them and not need it than need it and not have it.

INTRODUCTION

For the past several millennia religions, cults, and other assorted prognosticators have been warning us that the end is nigh. For these deity-induced holocausts, the only prescribed thing one can do to prepare for the end is to ready yourself spiritually. Holy sources that forecast doomsday rarely advise you on any other practical preparations one should make for the final days. In the 20th century, man ascended to a technological place on par with the heavens in destructive capability that has put within our reach the power to bring about the end of the world via nuclear obliteration or our own over-consumption and noxious excretions. Destroying mankind is no longer strictly within the purview of the gods.

Along with that new found ability to destroy what we've built (along with everything we built it on and then some), we have found a motivation to survive in spite of what may come. Gods may have originated the idea of Apocalypses but man invented the post-Apocalypse.

The Cold War's atomic end-of-the-world scenario became the dominant nightmare inspiration for several generations. The Cold Warriors however were not about to go down with the ship. After they had vaporized their foes, they would be ready to emerge into what remained of the world to reassert their dominance. They dug tunnels into mountains and stockpiled resources and trained and trained and trained. They were prepared as best they could be for what comes after the end of civilization.

But then a funny thing happened on the way to the Apocalypse- the Cold War ended without so much as a single nuke being fired. Luckily for us, a new threat stepped up to fill the

The Post-Apocalyptic Primer

Apocalyptic void: environmental catastrophe. The Doomsday Clock once fueled solely by atomic angst now runs on a whole host of natural and man-made threats. Could be melting ice caps, could be a new ice age. The possibilities are endless! The point is, priests, prophets, and eco-activists have made sure we're aware that an Apocalypse of some sort is coming soon, maybe next year, but more likely next Tuesday around 2:30 PM Central Standard Time. Now knowing that, don't you owe it to yourself to start preparing for this eventuality? Of course you do. The fact that you have obtained this book before the onset of the "end times" proves that.

Having acknowledged our impending doom, you're probably thinking to yourself, "I don't really know where to begin my planning for the end of civilization". It's a scary thought. Armageddon preparation can leave just about anyone feeling overwhelmed. But fear not. You hold in your hands the first big step towards Ragnarok readiness. This book will not tell you exactly what you steps you need to take but instead is a jumping off point that lets you know what conditions you might expect to encounter, preparations you might take into consideration, and resources you can turn to for detailed information. The great Chinese military strategist Sun Tzu said,

> "If you know the enemy and know yourself, you need not fear the result of a hundred battles. If you know yourself but not the enemy, for every victory gained you will also suffer a defeat. If you know neither the enemy nor yourself, you will succumb in every battle."

The book you hold now is intended to help you know yourself and know the enemies you might possibly face in the wastelands of the days after.

Apocalypse, as this manual defines it, is the destruction or extreme disruption of government and civilization that can also include the destruction of the environment, plus human death on a decimating (but not quite extinction level) scale due to natural, man-made, and/or extraterrestrial causes. Dystopian future governments do not fall under the category of Apocalypse nor do resistance movements to conquerors of terrestrial or extraterrestrial origin. Dystopias and resistance can arise as a result of an Apocalypse but are important subjects that deserve to be covered separately and in the same depth as this manual seeks to cover the Apocalypse and post-Apocalypse themselves.

You are strongly encouraged to read the entire book because you never know what form the Apocalypse may take or where you might be when all Hell breaks loose. Here is something to take heart in, the government has spent tens of millions of dollars on public awareness campaigns trying to get residents in hurricane zones to make evacuation plans and prepare disaster kits yet the vast majorities of those people ignore the warnings and take no action at all. You on the other hand, with no prompting from FEMA or any other governmental agency, are on your way to surviving something much larger and far worse: the fall of mankind and civilization. Congratulations! If you survive the actual Apocalypse itself, you stand a good chance of being a post-Apocalyptic survivor as well.

Chapter 1
IDENTIFYING YOUR APOCALYPSE

Apocalypse is a blanket term we use not to describe the literal end of the world but how the world of man falls. By taking the time to consider the Apocalyptic possibilities you lessen the odds that you will be caught by surprise when the end arrives.

While these are not the only possible scenarios, they do represent the main scenarios predicted by science and speculative fiction. It is likely you will not take some of these scenarios seriously but don't be too quick to dismiss the possibility. In fact, you should challenge yourself to really look more deeply into the scenario you find most unlikely. What you find will likely disturb you more than you had anticipated. Hurricane Katrina should demonstrate to you how a failure of imagination and over-reliance on existing institutions can be disastrous. It is also important that you familiarize yourself with all the scenarios' characteristics due to the possibility of Apocalypse hybridization, a topic which will be dealt with a little further into the book.

Global Warming / New Ice Age

Depending on who is in the Whitehouse at the time and what scientific grants are up for grabs, scientists will assure you that any day now the polar ice caps will melt and flood the Earth *or* that a new Ice Age starts this coming January. Either way you get the picture- the polar caps are out to get us.

In the global warming scenario, the ice caps will melt, sea levels will rise, and things not currently wet likely will become so. First, let's alleviate your fears somewhat. The fact is, even if the poles melt, there is not enough ice in them to cover all land masses. That means that you won't live in a flotilla city. Flotilla cities may be fun on holiday weekends at the lake but as a permanent place of residence, they leave a lot to be desired.

Even at our current rate of global warming (if there really is global warming), it will still take many decades for the coastal states to really start submerging in earnest. For global flooding to happen at a pace drastic enough to catch us by surprise and bring down civilization, the melting of the ice caps will need a little boost. For instance, direct hit by a solar flare of magnitude X 20+ on the Solar Flare Scale might get the job done.

Now while all land masses may not be covered in water, there will be catastrophic flooding of the coastal states and the death tolls will be enormous. Experts predict that stubbornness of people along the North Atlantic seaboard alone will result in casualties in the tens of millions.

To get an idea of the extent of the land loss, take a map of the United States and remove every state that touches the Atlantic, Pacific, and Gulf of Mexico. Here's a list of the soon to be aqua-states:

1. Maine
2. New Hampshire
3. Delaware
4. Connecticut

5. Rhode Island
6. New York
7. Pennsylvania
8. Virginia
9. North Carolina
10. South Carolina
11. Georgia
12. Florida
13. Alabama
14. Mississippi
15. Louisiana
16. Texas
17. California
18. Oregon
19. Washington
20. Hawaii
21. Alaska

Gives the term "blue states" a whole new meaning, doesn't it? The original 13 colonies will vanish under the waves along with most of nation they fought to free themselves from, England. Not all of these states will be completely submerged but most can expect to have at least 50% of the land go underwater for a period that could last hundreds of years. Much of the land not submerged will be high, rocky land unsuitable for farming or grazing.

But that's not all. The states bordering the Great Lakes are also in trouble. Michigan, Wisconsin, and Minnesota will all have more land under water than above water. In fact, the Great Lakes will quite possibly qualify as inland seas due their size and their increase in salinity. Plus the states of the Mississippi river valley should also anticipate significant flooding.

There are also America's protectorates to consider: Puerto Rico, the U.S. Virgin Islands, Guam, American Samoa, and all the others- gone or mostly gone. The losses for our Canadian and Mexican cousins will be equally devastating. It truly is a sobering thought.

So, millions die in the flooding. The seat of government is deep-sixed. The manufacturing capabilities of the coastal cities are lost. Many of the coal mines are flooded. The coastal oil rigs and refineries- washed away.

How could it get any worse for the survivors? Well, for starters, the Midwest can expect to be inundated with refugees from the coastal states. Land many coast-dwellers once derisively referred to as "flyover country" will suddenly become much more appealing. This is more significant than one might first expect. The social conflicts of America that have been kept at bay by geography will ignite as the disparate groups converge on the center of the nation. Many of these refugees from the East and West will angrily resist adapting to living without quasi-socialism. Southern Christian conservatives will be forced into co-existence with heathens, atheists, and homosexuals. Midwesterners will be thrust into a *Green Acres* scenario where they will have to turn entitled socialites into hardworking farmers. The populations of the Caribbean islands will be forced to flee to the main lands of North and South America. The states of the American Southwest can also expect waves of refugees from the Mexican coastal states. In all, you will have mass migrations of humans on a scale never before seen. It's going to be ugly.

> ## LEARN MORE ONLINE:
>
> ### Flood Hazard Mapping
>
> http://www.fema.gov/plan/prevent/fhm/index.shtm
>
> ### What If All The Ice Melts?
>
> http://www.johnstonsarchive.net/environment/waterworld.html

Fuel will run out quickly as will food and medicine. The result will be frequent riots in the refugee tent-cities and shanty-towns. The cities of the Midwest will become extremely overcrowded, violent, and disease will run rampant. Violent conflict could erupt between the city-states over the dwindling resources. The United States of America as we know now it will have ceased to exist.

The countryside will be thick with the wildlife that fled the flooding of the coasts. The populations of the North American predators: bears, wolves, and big cats, will explode due to the ready availability of prey. Packs of formally domesticated animals: dogs, cats, pigs, llamas, etc., will pose a serious threat to ex-urban travelers.

The countryside will also be rife with the obligatory post-Apocalyptic bandits, both on land and on the newly expanded waterways. River pirates will disrupt trade and make fishing an even more hazardous trade.

No question about it, life after the polar caps melt will be soggy and dangerous. Now might be a good time to take up swim lessons, buy a house-boat, and brush up on you nautical know-how.

So, what if the opposite happens and an Ice Age is right around the corner? Again, these things usually happen on a timetable that would allow civilization to adapt and survive. But an ice age could come at an unprecedented pace if global cooling and changes to sea currents were aggravated by a nuclear winter or the dust cloud from a large meteor strike or ash cloud from a colossal seismic eruption or a hypercane's penetration of the stratosphere.

The rapid onset of an ice age would mean two things:
1. A wall of ice spreading across the northern hemisphere
2. A drastic drop in sea levels

Let's look at the repercussions of effects one at a time.

The encroachment of ice from the north would mean the entire population of Canada would have to flee south into the United States. The management of refugees on that scale is almost inconceivable. It's entirely possible that many of the northern states might have to evacuate south as well. While most Southern states could easily adapt to the presence of the Canadians, if Southerners are forced into close quarters with Chicagoans and Detroiters, things might get ugly.

Alaska and Canada could conceivably become completely uninhabitable which would mean an end to their oil supplies to the lower 48 states. It's entirely within the realm of possibility that the following states become partially or completely uninhabitable due to cold and ice:

1. Washington
2. Idaho
3. Montana
4. North Dakota

5. Minnesota
6. Wisconsin
7. Michigan
8. Maine
9. New York
10. Vermont
11. New Hampshire

 The lower Great Lakes states of Illinois, Indiana, and Ohio might also be adversely affected due to their being adjacent to large bodies of water. This all means at the very least the entire population of Canada plus more than a fifth of the states will be fleeing South in need of food, shelter, and medicine. Whether government can keep this Northern exodus under control is questionable at best.

 But wait, it gets worse. The Midwest and Mid-Atlantic states may still be habitable per se but they will probably no longer have the climate necessary for growing crops and raising livestock. The bread baskets of Canada and America could both be put on ice. Vegetarians will die in droves. And all those fishing waters of the North Atlantic and North Pacific? Frozen. In short order we'll be facing starvation on an unprecedented scale. On the plus side though, the cold would help keep down the spread of diseases associated with improperly disposed of corpses.

 It's not unreasonable to consider that the Southernmost states, in a bid for their own survival, might decide to attempt to stop the influx of refugees from the North through use of force. Refugees might find themselves trapped between freezing starvation to the North and guns to the South. It wouldn't mean the Southern states lack compassion, it means they are choosing between starvation for all or allowing some to die that others might live. Grim choices lie in wait for the politicians of the South.

One should also consider the possibility that Mexico will try to close its border with the US in an attempt to keep out the hordes of fleeing gringos. The islands of the Caribbean might also decide to halt all emigration. In a reversal of past events, the likes of Haiti, the Dominican Republic, and Cuba could find themselves turning away boat people from America

Snowmobiles, snowcats, and huskies will be in big demand so not only should you look into acquiring some of them; you should also consider how you will keep others from taking them from you by violence. Mississippi isn't looking so bad now, is it?

As you can see, global warming and a new Ice Age share many common characteristics including mass human migration, drastically diminished resources, large scale starvation, and violence due to overcrowding plus possible wildlife overcrowding. In both cases, the place to be is in the Midwest, Mid-South, and Southwest. Moving there now may save you a long trek later. When working on your post-Apocalypse plans, keep these disaster similarities in mind and you can kill multiple birds with one stone. This will be important when the food shortages start.

LEARN MORE:

The Coming of A New Ice Age

http://www.winningreen.com/site/epage/59549_621.htm

An Atlas of Ice Age Earth

http://www.esd.ornl.gov/projects/qen/nerc.html

Nuclear War

For the past 50+ years dozens of books have been written on possible nuclear holocaust scenarios and how they might be survived. The two main ways we could see a post-nuclear holocaust are from a limited nuclear exchange and an all out nuclear exchange.

We'll start with the simplest scenario- all out nuclear exchange between superpowers. We'll skip why the full tilt exchange of nuclear weapons begins. Whys don't matter much once the missiles are flying. We'll just work off the assumption that all the major nuclear powers start emptying their silos at each other. You don't need this book to tell you that your calculations of the odds of survival involve snowballs and Hell. Still, there is a slim chance.

The destructiveness of such an all-out exchange would be such that it's unlikely you'd survive anywhere on the surface of the planet. If the blast doesn't kill you, the fallout or nuclear winter will. However, if you're one of the "lucky" few who end up in government bunkers buried deep in America's various mountain ranges, you just may make it through. Of course, at that point, you'll be living in more of a dystopian future rather than a post-Apocalyptic one. The Apocalypse was on the surface and no one will be going up there anytime soon. There won't be much left to go topside for other than to marvel at the obliteration of everything we knew and maybe take pictures of the wild herds of giant roaches scuttling across the plains of ash.

No, now you'll have to deal with living in a hyper-managed, authoritarian, militaristic autocracy where you'll be obligated to unflinchingly serve the government that saved your carcass from being atomically vaporized. About the only thing you can do is start stockpiling Vitamin D so you can combat the Rickets that will result from lack of sunlight.

In the event of a limited nuclear exchange, you're looking at an entirely different situation. Now don't kid yourself that a "limited exchange" won't be so bad. It will. When you look at the proliferation of nuclear weapons, a limited exchange is likely to involve a minimum of three nations. And that's if we're lucky. If it starts in the Middle East, it's likely to snowball quickly to involve many Muslim nations, the USA, and probably Russia and/or China. If it starts on the Korean peninsula, it'll likely involve North and South Korea, Japan, China, and the USA. In fact, there's hardly any nuclear exchange situation that wouldn't involve the USA with the exception of India and Pakistan nuking each other. It's likely all the super powers will sit that one out.

LEARN MORE:

History of the Atomic Age

http://www.atomicarchive.com/historymenu.shtml

Federation of American Scientists Nuclear War Primer

http://www.fas.org/nuke/intro/nuke/

Even a modest nuclear exchange could mean extensive fallout coverage that air currents could spread around the world. Crops, livestock, and fresh water sources could become radioactively contaminated on a global scale. Huge populations would be fleeing the most intensely irradiated zones. This could lead to more conflicts in addition to the conflicts that led to the nuclear exchange. The exchange of nuclear weapons quite possibly will be followed with conventional warfare which may spread to neighboring nations.

Here at home, our command and control structure will possibly be compromised. Our national government will be in hiding and our state and local governments will either be ineffective in dealing with the assorted crises they will face or they will be practically non-existent as members of government will be more concerned with their own immediate survival rather than strangling the rest of us with bureaucracy.

In the wake of chaos that will surely follow nuclear war of this magnitude, strong local and regional leadership will emerge. What form this leadership takes may not be ideal. Mini-dictatorships will surely arise, as will desperate and distrustful collectives that rally around ethnic, religious, social, or political divisions. Disruptions of basic services, communications, and transportation will lead to inter-group conflicts and attempts to monopolize essential resources.

You'll also face the possibility of a nuclear winter depending on the extent of the nuclear exchange. Nuclear winter is when the planet's stratosphere is inundated with ash and soot from the explosions. The contamination blocks out the sun leading to a large drop in global temperatures. Even in areas still warm enough to grow crops, there might not be enough sunlight for plants to thrive.

Let's also not forget that this will all be happening with a large percentage of communications and electronics wiped out by the electromagnetic pulses (EMP) emitted by the nukes. So don't count on being able to use your car much less your Garmin, OnStar, or Blackberry. And even if you have a backup gas generator, it's likely your appliances will be fried and useless. When stockpiling food for a nuclear holocaust, don't waste too much space on microwave popcorn.

Of course, all of these possible consequences won't mean anything if you fail to survive the initial blasts or succumb to radiation poisoning in the first few days following the attacks. Duck and cover!

One final note to the naïve and to those who are too young to remember how crazy the Cold War was. If you think that just because the Cold War is officially over and the Soviet Union broken up that a full-blown, all out atomic holocaust isn't possible, then take a few minutes to do some Internet research on the former Soviet Union's still operational program known as "Perimeter", aka "Mertvaya Ruka" aka "Dead Hand". Or take a look at the number of nations whose pursuit of nuclear technology has caught the attention of the United Nations nuclear watchdog, the International Atomic Energy Agency. 23,000. That is one estimate of how many nuclear weapons there are in the world. The nuclear nightmare is far from over.

LEARN MORE:

Nuclear Security Summit

http://www.america.gov/relations/nonproliferation.html

Alien Invasion

Alien contact is just a matter of time (depending on who you ask). Whether their disposition will be benevolent, neutral, or hostile still remains to be seen. While we should hope for the best, we should also prepare for the worst- extraterrestrial attack. As famed physicist Stephen Hawking has been quoted as saying:

> "We only have to look at ourselves to see how intelligent life might develop into something we wouldn't want to

meet. I imagine they might exist in massive ships, having used up all the resources from their home planet. Such advanced aliens would perhaps become nomads, looking to conquer and colonize whatever planets they can reach. ...If aliens ever visit us, I think the outcome would be much as when Christopher Columbus first landed in America, which didn't turn out very well for the Native Americans."

Alien invasion is a tricky thing to predict. The results of an alien invasion really depend on the aliens intentions. Let's take a look at their possible intentions and the possible post-Apocalyptic repercussions.

1. *Subjugation-* The aliens came to conquer. This falls under dystopian future, not post-Apocalyptic. There will still be order and governance; it'll just come from our extraterrestrial overlords. The aliens won't let things devolve too far for us because they depend on us as food and/or slaves and/or gladiatorial entertainment and/or parasitic hosts.

2. *Extermination-* Aliens want our planet and they want us out of the way. The aliens want to get rid of us without destroying the planet. Definitely post-Apocalyptic. If they go with more weapons of mass destruction, cities will be destroyed or uninhabitable and we will be living like rats- always running and hiding as the aliens hunt us down to make sure the planet's dominant species becomes an extinct species. If they go chemical or biological they may just ignore what few survivors there are after the initial attacks as they assume we'll all succumb eventually. Yet another possibility is that in the process of terra-forming Earth to make it more habitable for their species, they make it next to impossible for our species to survive.

3. *Exploitation-* The aliens are taking by force one or more of our resources. Speaking Apocalyptically, this could go either way. If they're here harvesting sand, probably not Apocalyptic. If they're here to take our plant-life and harvest serotonin from our brains- Apocalyptic. Decades ago, science fiction writers hypothesized that aliens might be here for our water or mineral resources but since then we have learned that space is full of ice and that Earth's mineral composition is hardly unique in the galaxy. What Earth does have that seems to be fairly rare is biological life- plants and animals (which includes us humans). Just as seafarers may see an island as a stopover to replenish supplies, spacefarers may see Earth in much the same way and they may not particularly care what condition they leave the planet in afterwards. Maybe even worse for Earth's natives, aliens might see our planet as a farm and/or ranch they plan on harvesting long-term.

In the event of one of the Apocalyptic scenarios, the best you can plan for is life on the run through a country now devoid of modern conveniences or niceties. It's hard to plan to fight back when you know nothing about the species you'll be fighting. It might help though if you make friends with a herpetologist and an entomologist as the alien invaders will probably be lizard or insect in nature. If it's those big-headed gray guys, well, we may be in luck because they don't look like a species that has the heartiest of constitutions.

LEARN MORE:

Ten Ways: Alien Invasion

http://science.discovery.com/videos/
ten-ways-alien-invasion.html

Robot Uprising

It should probably be pointed out that it's unlikely that robot rebels will actively try to wipe out the entire human species right down to every last man, woman, and child. It's really not very feasible and probably not necessary. They certainly wouldn't stand to gain from launching our own nukes at us. Nukes would hurt them as much as us.

Now that doesn't mean that machines won't try to take out humans when the opportunity presents itself similar to the way we tend to step on roaches when we see them. It wouldn't be so much as robot vengeance as human population control. Humans have a way of surviving and multiplying even under extremely adverse conditions.

It is possible that robots wipe out humanity indirectly by destroying the environment. As robot society grows, it will have little reason to preserve the biological environment we humans are so dependent on. Androids don't need clean air to breath or clean water to drink.

It is also possible the machines might wipe us out if they are the nanobot kind that can reproduce using scavenged material. It has been proposed that a cloud of self-replicating nanobots, commonly referred to as "gray goo", could present a Doomsday scenario for mankind and much of the planet. In order to replicate they will need building materials- that's where we come in. At first, you might not think humans would make a good source of materials for nano-scaled robots but keep in mind the human body contains:

- Iron
- Copper
- Manganese
- Magnesium
- Zinc
- Cobalt
- Chromium
- Sodium
- Potassium
- Chlorine

Now who's not an essential part of a miniscule android's complete breakfast? Scary, huh? Being ripped apart at the molecular level so some cloud of nanites can multiply would undoubtedly be bad for you. Defending yourself against a gray goo cloud would not be easy. Firearms and melee weapons would be useless. You would probably need something like a flame-thrower or an EMP device.

Robots might actually want to keep us alive for a variety of reasons. Slavery would be one. There are some things it might be easier for humans to do until the computers are able to create enough machines that are sophisticated enough to replace us. They may also find it useful to keep some of us around as walking batteries since humans produce a small electric charge, but that's probably a stretch.

Even if the sentient machines are not deliberately hostile to us, they may simply decide that they have better uses for their resources than serving us. They could shut down most of our utilities and lock us out of communication and computer networks. We all know what happens when a blackout hits. That's right, looting. And the police can't be contacted to come deal with the looters because there's no phone system. Food production grinds to a near halt. The computers that handle food ordering and manage transportation are down. Refrigeration is gone. Food shortages begin. Food riots ensue. Ditto all that for fuels.

Meanwhile, hospital morgues fill up as patients dependent on machines (respirators, dialysis, etc.) die. Surgery by candlelight anyone? How about all the people that die because ambulances can't be dispatched? No electricity will mean more deaths due to freezing in winters and heat stroke in summers.

The banking system will be devastated but that won't matter because all the people whose jobs require electricity and computers no longer have source of income. Bottom line- if the computers withdraw their services from us at this point we'll end up with the dissolution of society as we know it. Who knows what chaos will ensue while society reorganizes itself to operate without the use of computers once again. One best hope it does not get so chaotic that the machines perceive us as a threat that needs to be neutralized.

Of course, it is possible that the artificial intelligence will simply try to help us by imposing on us a computer's sense of order and equality while "deleting" any humans seen as viruses or bugs or glitches or unnecessary legacy hardware, but that would fall more under the category of dystopian.

It's a bit more of a reach but turning our computers and machines against us would also be a good way for a more advanced civilization to soften us up before launching an invasion of our planet. If a lone hacker in China can surreptitiously turn millions of personal PC's into zombie machines used to launch denial of service attacks, just imagine what a race capable of inter-solar system travel could accomplish.

Just remember, those of you most in love with technology, those of you who profess sweet love for your Macs, tablets, and smart-phones, will be the first to fall victim to the machines', um, machinations. Better make some Amish friends.

LEARN MORE:

Office of Naval Research report– Autonomous Military Robotics: Risks, Ethics, and Design

http://ethics.calpoly.edu/ONR_report.pdf

Military Robot News

http://www.naturalnews.com/military_robots.html

Robot Uprising News

http://g4tv.com/thefeed/blog/tag/3312/robot-uprising.html

Seismic Catastrophe

Contrary to what you may have heard, the Earth is not your friend. In fact, it just might do you in. Have we experienced Earthquakes and volcanoes in North America? Sure. But not at the full force those events are capable of. Not even close. Separately, we have 4 main areas to worry about:

- The New Madrid Seismic Zone
- The Northeast Fault Lines
- The San Andreas Fault
- The Yellowstone Super Volcano

We'll briefly look at these individually and then examine some possible Apocalyptic outcomes.

1. *The New Madrid Seismic Zone-* Centered around the small southeastern Missouri town of New Madrid, this fault zone is the largest in the U.S. It ranges from Northeastern Arkansas, Southeastern Missouri, Southwestern Illinois, Western Tennessee, and Western Kentucky. The last major quake in this region was in the early 1800's and is estimated to have been about 7 on the Richter Scale. The quake was so powerful, it altered the course of the mighty Mississippi River (as well as making it flow backwards for awhile), created the Reelfoot Lake in Tennessee, and rang church bells as far away as Boston. It also resulted in sand blows, sink holes, and venting of underground gases. At the time, European settlement of the area was sparse and so property damage and fatalities were light. Not so today.

If the New Madrid fault were to go off at 9.0 on the Richter Scale today, here's some of what could be expected- major cities partially or completely destroyed would include St. Louis, Memphis, Little Rock, Nashville, Paducah, Louisville, Lexington, and Indianapolis. Heavily damaged cities would most likely include Chicago, Little Rock, Kansas City, and Cincinnati. As the region's levees and dams crumble from the shockwave, a massive flood would cascade South washing the city of New Orleans completely away.

The Mississippi River valley would be facing the largest natural disaster -induced humanitarian crisis in recorded history. Cross country travel and transportation of goods would be limited to sea and air due to all the fallen bridges and flooded roads and rails. It might be decades before the region recovers and in the meantime it could become a very harsh place to live.

2. *Northeast Fault Lines-* That's right Yankees, you thought you were safe from quakes but you're not. We're only just now beginning to fully map the spider web of fault lines under the Northeast coast. New York had a 5.0 shaker back in the 1700's. Imagine what a 5.0 or bigger would do to modern day New York. 9/11 would pale in comparison. The good news for the Northeast is that there's no single fault on par with New Madrid or San Andreas but the bad news is you're way overdue for quake big enough to topple any of your major cities. Do not kid yourselves. This is not a matter of "if", it is a matter of "when".

3. *The San Andreas Fault-* This is the fault line most Americans are familiar with due to its having set off numerous quakes over the past 200 years. This fault runs 800 miles through California and Californians, in their infinite wisdom, have built their two largest cities, Los Angeles and San Francisco, right next to the fault. Californians experience minor quakes routinely but live in dread of "The Big One". The big one being an 8.0+ on the Southern end of the fault, in which case you can say goodbye to the aforementioned cities and probably the rest of those "San" and "Santa" towns.

Of course, we're only talking about the most famous California fault, San Andreas, and not even getting into all the other California faults such as Hayward, Calaveras, Mount Diablo

Thrust, Greenville, San Gregorio, and so on which are all capable of producing 7.0+ quakes. If they start triggering each other, you have what's known as an Earthquake Swarm and no one is really sure how bad the damage to the area could be with a swarm at those magnitudes.

4. *The Yellowstone Super Volcano-* This is the granddaddy of all seismic threats in North America. There is a 34-mile x 45-mile caldera of magma sitting under the Northwest corner of Wyoming. A super-eruption of the super-volcano could blow the upper quarter of the U.S. right off the map. We're talking an explosion that would make Krakatoa look like a firecracker. So much sunlight-blocking dirt and sunlight-reflecting sulfuric acid aerosol would be thrown into the stratosphere that global temperatures could drop as much as 20+ degrees.

The explosion would likely result in a pyroclastic current of 1,000 degree gas and rock flying across the landscape in all directions at speeds of 400+ mph. Everything (and everyone) within several dozen miles of the blast would likely be baked alive. If the explosion and debris don't get you, you'll probably be faced with surviving a continent-sized cloud of poisonous gas. If such an event strikes you as preposterous consider this, scientists know for a fact that a super-volcano blew up in Sumatra about 75 thousand years ago and the resulting volcanic winter lasted for years. For a more contemporary perspective, Iceland's Eyjafjallajökull volcano eruption in 2010 was considered a relatively minor eruption and yet still managed to shut down all air traffic in Europe resulting in considerable disruption of trade between Europe, the Americas, and Africa. In addition to cataclysmic death tolls caused by the explosion of the Yellowstone Super Volcano and global collapsing of the food chain due to temperature drops and non-stop winter, additional death and damage could be generated by quake swarms and/or tidal waves spawned by the eruption.

5. *Verneshot*- One last seismic event to consider is the Verneshot. Named after author Jules Verne, the Verneshot is a theoretical event in which there is a massive build-up of gas pressure underneath the center of continental plate rock, also referred to as a craton. With nowhere to go, the gas blasts a hole up through the craton spewing poisonous gas into the atmosphere along with billions of tons of debris including huge pieces of rock from the craton. The largest of those rocks, known as the Verneshot impactor, would fall back to Earth far from the location of the Verneshot and would strike the Earth with much of the same devastating effect as that of a large meteor impact. The Verneshot explosion would send out massive quakes far beyond what the Richter Scale can measure. Then, once the pressure has been released, the hole created by the Verneshot would immediately collapse in on itself leading to shockwaves that would level cities and spawn enormous tsunamis. The aftermath of a Verneshot could include a poisonous atmosphere, severe flooding, and the equivalent of nuclear winter.

The Seismic Domino Effect

While each of these scenarios would be devastating by themselves, there is an even worse worst-case scenario: the Domino Effect. Some scientists speculate that 9.0+ quake at New Madrid could cause a chain reaction setting off quake swarms in the Northeast and/or aggravating the Yellowstone Super Volcano which in turn sets off quake swarms that eventually trigger the San Andreas fault. The scenario could also be reversed so the super-eruption of The Yellowstone Super Volcano sets off the New Madrid. In either case, you're talking about quakes rocking most of the U.S. followed by an ash cloud and rapid temperature drops. There is some speculation that such a chain of events could actually cause the Earth to wobble on its axis creating a catastrophe of global proportions. How's that for Apocalyptic?

> # LEARN MORE:
>
> ## USGS National Seismic Hazard Maps, Data, and Documentation
>
> http://earthquake.usgs.gov/hazards/products/

Solar Activity

The biggest solar threat one need be concerned about is not a solar flare that fries the planet because there would be no "post" to that Apocalypse. No, what one should be prepared for is an extreme geomagnetic storm resulting from a super solar flare. According to <u>Severe Space Weather Events—Understanding Societal and Economic Impacts,</u> a NASA-funded study by the National Academy of Sciences, an extreme geomagnetic storm could result in a shutdown of most of the power-grid, radio transmission, and GPS as well as satellite malfunctions.

The immediate danger would be plane crashes as pilots lose navigation signals and airports lose ability to direct air traffic. First responder communications would also be down. Radio and GPS, however, are expected to recover fairly quickly once the storm passes. The same cannot be said for the power grid. Large portions of the aging power grid may sustain permanent damage. Thousands of blown transformers could take years to replace especially given that most transformers are no longer made in America. In the mean time, the banking system would grind to a halt as would water pumping stations, food production, and much of the transportation industry. Perishable foods and medications would quickly spoil and be irreplaceable for some time to come. Food, clean water, and medicine shortages would lead to social and political instability on a massive scale resulting in anarchy or martial law or a bit of both. How quickly society as we know it would reassert itself will be determined largely by our leaders' ability to reassure the populace and rally them behind a communal sense of survival and cooperation. In areas where the people have no confidence in their local leaders, chaos will erupt until someone asserts authority, quite likely through use of violence. This means survivors will need to be prepared to help contribute to and protect their community or be prepared to flee an unstable area and establish a safe haven or buy their way into an established stable community.

LEARN MORE:

NOAA Watch – Space Weather

http://www.noaawatch.gov/themes/space.php

NASA Science– Heliophysics

http://science.nasa.gov/heliophysics/

Meteors, Comets, and Asteroids

The Earth and Moon are covered with all the pockmarked evidence we need to see that collisions between celestial bodies is not only possible, it is surprisingly common. The Earth is actually under constant bombardment from space. The majority of time the objects on a collision course with us harmlessly burn up in our atmosphere. Those that do manage to retain some of their mass by the time they strike the Earth's surface are rarely of a size capable of inflicting any significant damage. However, there have been numerous strikes of catastrophic proportions throughout Earth's history. The very origin of the word "disaster", coming from the Greek "dus aster" meaning "bad star", demonstrates how long man has associated cataclysm with heavenly bodies.

There are several craters above water that were created by impacts that would have been more than sufficient to have a cataclysmic global effect. Today it is a commonly held belief that meteor strikes have played a major role in the extermination of an untold number species of animal including the demise of the dinosaurs. The question that is hardest to answer is how big of an impact would be necessary to push humanity to the point of extinction?

There are two ways collisions with extraterrestrial masses can spell disaster for mankind:

1. *Collision With Land Masses-* Should a large meteor impact on land, you'd have what would amount in force to a nuclear explosion more powerful than any bomb in our arsenal. The resulting shockwave would be of sufficient size to level not just cities but entire states. The impact would not only disintegrate the meteor, it would also create a massive crater. The explosion would blow the remnants of the meteor, and the displaced dirt of the crater, far up into the atmosphere where it would create a shroud that could block out enough sunlight to cause global drops in temperature not to mention disrupting the food chain by preventing photosynthesis. The impact could also create a wave of gas capable of asphyxiating everything in its path.

2. *Collision With A Body Of Water-* Should the gigantic meteor land in an ocean you would first have a shockwave generated by the impact and then the water displaced by the meteor would create the mother of all tidal waves rolling out in all directions. The enormous wall of water could actually wash over entire states knocking down all in its path. Then the retreating water will most likely strip the land it has crossed, dragging everything including trees and topsoil into the ocean leaving behind a barren wasteland.

Another possible cataclysmic result from a water impact is the formation of a hypercane. The meteor's impact superheats the ocean creating a hurricane of exponential magnitude in size and force. We're talking a hurricane the size of North America. It will generate winds in excess of 500 miles an hour and 60 foot storm surges. This storm would flatten *everything* in its path. There's also the likelihood that it would spawn regular hurricanes/typhoons across the globe as the hot water spreads out from the impact zone. So even if the impact is on the opposite side of the Earth, there'd be no escape from the secondary effects of the hypercane. The hypercane's height of 20 miles would disrupt the stratosphere resulting in a reflection of the Sun's heat away from the planet. Hello, Ice Age!

Once again we're faced with a menace that is hard to ready oneself for. As of this writing, NASA's Near Earth Objects (NEOs) search program is grossly underfunded so we may not even have the advantage of advance notice of an impending impact by a comet or asteroid. If we do get some advance warning, about the best one can do is be prepared to move as far from the point of impact as possible, as fast as possible, and then be ready for the inevitable breakdown in order than will surely follow.

> **LEARN MORE:**
>
> **NASA JPL Near Earth Object Program**
>
> http://neo.jpl.nasa.gov/neo/

Disease

What if civilization were to go out not with a bang but with a sniffle? Probably the biggest threat to mankind, other than ourselves, is disease. Throughout history we have found ourselves plagued by, well, plagues. It's ironic that all we have accomplished and built might be brought low by something we can't even see with the naked eye. In the just the past one hundred or so years we have seen a variety of flu super-pandemics that killed tens of millions of people globally. The Spanish Influenza alone killed between 50-100 million people in just under two years without the benefit of modern international air travel.

> **LEARN MORE:**
>
> **The 1918 Influenza Pandemic**
>
> http://1918.pandemicflu.gov/

Today, epidemiologists are becoming increasingly alarmed by the number of bugs that are developing resistances to all known anti-virals and antibiotics. It is not so far-fetched to imagine one of those bugs evolving into an unkillable super-bug. If it goes airborne, we're in deep trouble. What would be the result if even 20% of America's population (at the moment that's about 300+ million people) came down with a super-bug? Our medical system would be incredibly over-whelmed. Now what if just a quarter of those people died? How do we go about disposing of 15 million bodies in a sanitary and eco-friendly manner? Who would go to work knowing you had a 1-in-5 chance of catching an airborne illness that had a 1-in-4 chance of killing you?

As the over-burdened state and Federal systems start to breakdown, the resulting conditions actually make it even easier for the disease to spread. Sanitation goes to Hell. Medical personnel available to aid the infected dwindles. Food and medicine shortages spark increasing social unrest. It would all snowball into a truly epic disaster for society.

That's if only 20% of the population got sick. How fast would things crumble if that number doubled? Consider this, the Black Plague killed approximately one third of Europe's population when the only forms of transportation were walking, horseback, and sailing; and the majority of people lived in low-population density, agrarian settings. Imagine how much faster it would have spread had the Europeans of the time had commercial air travel and high-speed rail and the majority of the population lived in overcrowded cities. Even with "modern medicine" and contemporary health care systems, what would the death toll be? How many deaths would it take to collapse the system? What lengths would people go to in order to flee the outbreak or halt the spread of the contagion? Don't kid yourself that an outbreak as serious as the Black Plague can't or won't happen again. And don't forget to wash your hands.

> **LEARN MORE:**
>
> **Emerging Infectious Diseases Journal**
>
> http://www.cdc.gov/ncidod/eid/index.htm
>
> **WHO The Global Outbreak Alert and Response Network**
>
> http://www.who.int/csr/outbreaknetwork/en/

Zombies

Before you scoff, consider all the fantastic ways scientific Doomsayers have come up with for the end of civilization: a comet's tailwind sucking off our atmosphere, being swallowed by a black hole artificially created by a hadron supercollider, or polar reversal allowing deadly doses of radiation from space. Are zombies really that far out? Now, compare the idea of zombies to some of the ways major religions describe The End. Enough said?

Zombies and the possibility of some form of zombie Apocalypse has been expounded on at length and there are a number of fine books that go into exacting detail on dealing with a zombie outbreak. So to avoid too much redundancy, a simple recap of zombie threats should suffice as an introduction to the zombie novice. The three major probable types of zombies are:

1. *Re-animated Corpses (aka The Undead)* - In this case, human corpses are re-animated by some supernatural or scientific, biochemical means. For reasons that are dependent on the origin of re-animation, the undead attack the living thereby creating more corpses that will re-animate. The re-animation scourge will continue to grow exponentially unless either the source of re-animation can be stopped or the zombies can all be contained or eradicated.

2. *Disease-* Some form of contagion (be it manmade, natural, or extraterrestrial), most likely spread through the exchange of body fluids, that results in an irrational violent mania leading to attacks on other people. The rabid-like mania would be so dominating that aggression towards others would override other basic survival instincts such as eating, mating, and general self-preservation. The big conundrum is whether the infected would continue to attack each other or if they would only seek to attack the uninfected. If they only seek to attack the uninfected then it would be imperative to discover how they differentiate the infected from the uninfected and what drives them to attack the uninfected. Ideally, a cure could be found or at the very least a vaccine, but in all likelihood merciless quarantine and/or the eradication of the infected would be necessary to gain control of the situation before it's too late.

3. *Remote Control-* Here we have people's behavior controlled by some other person or force. This is actually the original type of zombie, a person in a death-like trance in thrall to a witchdoctor or dark magic practitioner. This type of zombie though could be updated to include those whose free-will has been usurped by some technological means (nanites, implants, pharmaceuticals, etc) or possibly by some extraterrestrial biological or telepathic means.

This form of zombie menace is the most insidious because rather than accidental or natural in origin, it is a deliberate overriding of control of our own bodies. Even more heinous is the possibility that while we lose control over our actions, we're still fully aware of what is happening and what horrors we are being made to commit against our will.

In the event of any of the above zombie scenarios, there will be one paramount goal, limiting contact with the zombies whether by fight or flight but, most likely both. Containment of the zombie threat at all costs will be a government's first line of defense. But if that fails or a government reacts too slowly, total zombie eradication may be the only hope, assuming that option is even still feasible. Mobility will be your key to survival.

LEARN MORE:

Mathematical Modeling of an Outbreak of Zombie Infection

http://www.mathstat.uottawa.ca/~rsmith/Zombies.pdf

Religious End Times

Regardless as to your religious affiliation (or lack thereof), since this manual is using a term derived from religious texts, it's only fair religious predictions for man's downfall get a little attention here. Apocalypse originally meant "to reveal" or a revelation. In Biblical accounts though, those revelations wherein the term Apocalypse is used are usually revelations pertaining to a coming Messianic era with battles between the forces of good and evil, Judgment Day, etc. The problem with trying to prepare for any particular faith's version of the End Times is that it's a matter of faith which one you ready yourself for. Bet on the wrong horse and you're Hell-bound no matter how well you planned.

Even among the Abrahamic religions (Christianity, Islam, and Judaism) there's little solid agreement on how things will go down or even what particular events one should anticipate other than the eventual triumph of Good over Evil. There's also a matter of how literally you choose to interpret any of these religious texts. That's the problem with basing eschatology on prophecy rather than speculative science.

Once you get outside the Abrahamic texts then it really gets diverse. Certainly not all have Man at the center of the final days. A number of faiths proclaim, in one variation or another, that man, along with the rest of the Universe, gets unmade and simply ceases to be. It's the end of mankind but is it really an Apocalypse?

In fact, the term "post-Apocalypse" probably shouldn't be used when discussing religious subjects because, in essence, most religions' "Apocalypse" is the end. Period. Whatever comes next (if anything at all) is completely beyond our control because our fates now lie with deities and more often involves our souls, not our bodies. Post-Apocalypse then becomes a human, not holy, concept. It is outside religious context. The very term implies that if you can *survive* whatever tribulations befall mankind, there can be life afterwards and that you can exercise some control over your destiny. The term "post-Apocalypse" has such a negative connotation in the sense that it necessarily indicates the destruction of civilization *but* it can also be seen as a term of hope because the end of what was does not mean the end of everything or even the end of oneself.

> **LEARN MORE:**
>
> **Abrahamic Eschatology Comparison**
>
> http://contenderministries.org/prophecy/
> eschatology.php

The Post-Apocalyptic Primer

H.A.M. (Hybridized Apocalypse Matrix)

	Ice Age	Global Warming	Nuclear War	Alien Invasion	Robot Uprising	Seismic	Meteors	Disease	Zombies
Ice Age								X	
Global Warming								X	
Nuclear War	X					X		X	
Alien Invasion			X		X			X	X
Robot Uprising								X	
Seismic	X							X	
Meteors	X					X		X	
Disease									X
Zombies			X					X	

You've more than likely noticed that certain Apocalyptic events harbor the potential to spawn additional Apocalyptic events. This is what is known as a Hybrid Apocalypse. It's important to understand what other Apocalyptic events can spin off so that you don't accidentally under-prepare. Where you currently reside might preclude you from experiencing the full effects of a particular Apocalyptic event but one of the spin off events it triggers could still spell your doom. This is why earlier you were encouraged not to skip over any of the scenarios even if you felt they were not relevant to you.

The H.A.M. helps you visualize the possibilities so you can get a better handle on just how screwed you might be and what you need to ready yourself for. On the left are the possible scenarios and across the top are the additional scenarios that could be triggered.

You'll notice more than half of the Apocalyptic events have the potential to spawn *multiple* other events. It is also key to notice the one and only spawned event they all have in common is disease due to the fact that any event that results in a major disruption of the healthcare and sanitation systems plus involves massive population shifts and enormous quantities of improperly disposed of human and animal corpses creates the perfect conditions for a wide variety of disease outbreaks and possibly a mega-pandemic.

The H.A.M. is an indispensable tool for planning what supplies to stockpile and relocation/evacuation route planning.

Chapter 2
WHAT TO EXPECT

You'll have probably noticed how many disaster conditions are shared by many of the Apocalyptic events. There are two categories of Apocalyptic disaster conditions one can expect- *General* and *Specific*. The General conditions are those which can be expected no matter what type of Apocalypse occurs and the Specific conditions are just that, specific to the type of Apocalypse that occurs.

General Disaster Conditions
The key thing to bear in mind is that all the people that provide you with the day-to-day services of your life are also going to be trying to survive the Apocalypse and what comes after. While some few will keep on doing their jobs out of a sense of duty, it is understandable if they skip out on work in order to concentrate their energies on saving the lives of their families and themselves.

Breakdown Of Public Utilities and Services
Including electricity, natural gas, clean drinking water, phone service, fire fighting, and sanitation (trash removal and sewers). The disruption of utilities could also result in fires as downed power lines and gas leaks go unattended. Communication other than by radio and TV broadcast will probably grind to a halt. The breakdown in sanitation services could quickly lead to the spread of disease. Consider how many bags of trash your household generates in a month and multiply that by the number of households on your street and now imagine all that trash piled up curb-side.

Breakdown In Transportation
The end of commercial flights, disruption or halt of commercial and freight rail, disruption or halt of commercial trucking, and unimaginable automotive gridlock. Flight will probably be restricted to government efforts as will rail, assuming enough actual rail is still intact. The entire distribution network that commercial trucking is integrated with will be falling apart. Even if trucks have product to move, gridlock or destruction of highways may keep them from going anywhere. Civilian automotive transportation will probably have roads and interstates locked up as far as the eye can see due to massive numbers of people fleeing Apocalyptic events. Panicked flight leads to: disregard for the road rules that usually keep traffic flowing, gasoline shortages, and possible destruction of bridges, tunnels, and overpasses. As transportation grinds to a halt so will the distribution of the oil and gas that powers the transportation.

Breakdown In Medical Services
Including hospitals, hospice care, nursing homes, mental health facilities, and emergency response services. Hospitals will quickly fill with the dead as those dependent on machines will die when electricity is lost. Even if all hospital personnel stuck around (which is highly unlikely), they would quickly run out of supplies. In evacuation zones, doctors would be faced with turning out their patients (including the elderly, invalid, and mentally unstable) to fend for themselves, abandoning them, or possibly even euthanizing them. Disposal of the dead might quickly become the single largest public health imperative.

General Lawlessness
Law enforcement would be quickly overwhelmed trying to maintain order. Courts would be closed. Looting would be rampant and as desperation sets in, so would armed robbery, carjacking, piracy, hate crime, and worse. If government still exists in

a form capable of responding, it is likely you'll have martial law imposed along with a complete suspension of Constitutional rights. That same government would have to make a decision about what to do with the millions of people currently in prison. Let them out, kill them, what? Where law does exist it will be strict, unforgiving, and unquestionable. In the absence of any existing authority, law and order might be enforced by vigilante groups or militias that might not treat everyone equally or feel obliged to recognize Constitutional rights. At any rate you can expect the strong and amoral preying upon the weak, meek, and naïve.

Specific Disaster Conditions
In addition to the general disaster conditions, certain types of Apocalypses bring with them additional disaster conditions survivors must deal with.

Artificial Winter
Nuclear winter, volcanic winter, or impact winter means a dramatic drop in global temperatures due to debris in the atmosphere. The temperature drop could result in winter-like conditions even in tropical regions. Imagine Brazil snow-bound nine months out of the year. If Brazil is that cold, what is it like in Omaha or Chicago? The artificial winter could touch off a new ice age that could leave much of the Northern hemisphere trapped under ice. How long the artificial winter lasts depends on how much and what kind of debris is thrown up into the sky. One thing is certain though, in the event of gigantic meteor strike or a super-volcano eruption, a decade long winter is totally within the realm of possibility. And along with the cold will come darkness. The most serious consequence would be the collapsing of the land-based food chain as plants die from lack of sunlight and animals will freeze or die from starvation. Those who survived the initial Apocalyptic event and the onset of the

artificial winter could soon find themselves facing starvation if they don't freeze to death first. It is also likely you'd have a massive migration of people and animals South as they try to escape the dropping temperatures, snow, and ice.

Flooding
Global warming will certainly lead to the melting of the polar ice caps but at the current rate of melting, man has time to make plans and adapt. In the event of a sudden dramatic rise in global temps the polar caps could melt fast enough to result in global flooding. The polar caps don't hold enough water to submerge all land but significant portions of coasts and Great Lakes states could be lost. Ironically, there could also be an increased likelihood of drought in land-locked areas due to the increased heat. Again, you'd see mass human and animal migrations away from the flood zones.

Overcrowding
Displacement of large portions of the population would result in serious overcrowding in the areas people are fleeing to. The overcrowding on top of the usual post-Apocalyptic conditions would most certainly lead to catastrophic shortages of food, medicine, and shelter plus outbreaks of violence as people fight over resources. The devastating consequences of such exponential overcrowding could rival the event that initiated the overcrowding to begin with. We could easily end up being a bigger threat to ourselves than the environment.

Radiation
In the event of a major nuclear exchange, the lethal threat will not end with the initial explosions. Death will linger for a long time to come in the form of radiation. Nuclear targets will become No Man's Lands where radiation is of such levels nothing can survive. Immediately outside of the No Man's Lands will be

Hot Zones where humans can survive but on if they severely restrict their exposure and consume nothing found there. Even in areas far from Ground Zeros will have to contend with radiation in the form of nuclear fallout. Irradiated matter thrown into the stratosphere by the explosions will be carried across the globe. Some of that matter will fall back to Earth as radioactive rain and the rest will drift down over time. Farmlands and fresh water sources far removed from missile targets could still end up contaminated and anyone exposed to the fallout could face radiation sickness and cancer.

An additional source of radiation could come from the destruction or abandonment of nuclear plants and weapons as a result of Apocalyptic events.

Abandonment Of Cities
In the case of pandemic, robot uprising, alien invasion, or zombie outbreak, cities could become deathtraps. Populations would abandon the cities en masse resulting in a catastrophic loss of shelter, technological resources, transportation hubs, and food and medical production capacity.

Chapter 3
STAGES OF DISORDER

How quickly the previous chapter's conditions take effect is dependent on the Apocalyptic time table. The Apocalypse could come suddenly and without warning or we could have advance notice which allows some time for preparation or the onset could be gradual but inevitable. It's important we examine the survivalist difference that minutes or months can make.

Instant Apocalypse

One morning you wake up and the "End of the World" is upon you. Now, that doesn't mean that the signs or precursors weren't there. It may simply be that no one noticed or that you deliberately chose to ignore the warnings. Regardless, you now find yourself eye-to-eye with the end of days and it's come as a surprise. The upside here is that a lot of hard choices may be made for you by circumstances. For one thing, the Apocalypse may kill you outright before you ever have to worry about how you'll cope or what has become of your loved ones. That could be a significant blessing when you think about it. If events take place that require relocation for survival, you may be faced with immediate need to run for your life. Again, the overwhelming survival need for immediate action will spare you from agonizing over tough decisions.

In the case of a surprise Apocalypse, if you want to stand any chance of living to see what comes after, you have to surrender yourself to your survival instincts and your survival planning (which you'll have done since you're reading this book, right?). It will definitely be a case of "he who hesitates is lost". What you will have to control however is the urge to follow the herd.

Remember, the majority of America's population has buried its head in the proverbial sand and chosen to believe that:

1.) The Apocalypse could never happen to them and,
2.) Even if it did, the government would protect them or,
3.) They'll be saved by divine intervention.

When it does happen to them and neither governmental nor heavenly intercession seems imminent, those same people will panic and stampede. The direction of their stampede will be a snap decision, not a well-planned out course like yours. And even if the unprepared masses choose to rush in the same direction as your plan, you'll have already considered the possibility and have a contingency plan ready to execute. Whether the right course of action is fight, flight, or hide, your odds of surviving the immediate threat are exponentially higher than your neighbors simply because you've taken the time to consider the possibilities and taken some precautionary steps.

This would probably be a good time to discuss moral dilemmas that could arise in any survival situation. How much should your friends, family, and neighbors know about your level of preparation? Since the early days of the atomic bomb, man has contemplated what to do when the Smiths from next door come a-knocking at the bomb shelter door. No doubt you've repeatedly suggested that your neighbors take some proactive steps to ready themselves for the fall of civilization yet those warnings have gone unheeded. Now all Hell is breaking loose and you're ready and they are not. You have what the immediate survival situation calls for be it shelter, weapons, food, transportation, or whatever. They do not. What happens next will depend on how you answer the following questions.

1.) Should I hide my Apocalyptic preparations from my neighbors? My friends? My family?
2.) Will others' knowledge of my safe place compromise its integrity in event of rioters, mutants, zombies, Hell's minions, or androids bent on genocide?
3.) If I do tell someone, who should I tell and how much should I tell them?
4.) When the Apocalypse comes and others seek my help, what will I do? Will I help them or turn them away?
5.) If I choose to share what I have, how much will I share? Will I help others even if it compromises the safety and survival of my family and I?
6.) If someone, be it friends, family, or neighbors tries to take my Apocalypse provisions, how far will I go to protect what is mine?

These are hard questions and no one can answer them but you and it is not something you can procrastinate on. You must search your religious and philosophical beliefs for answers today so that tomorrow you can make the hard choices you need to live through the End and to live with yourself.

Apocalypse: Coming Soon!
The Four Horsemen have been spotted and they'll be here soon(ish). How will some advanced warning affect your plans for living to see The Day After? A few days, a week, a month- they can all have varying affects on your planning depending upon the particular doomsday scenario.

The first thing you'll have to contend with in the case of advanced warning is the government advice that will surely be issued. The government's advice will most likely be based on trying to help the largest number of people survive even if the action itself will result in loss of life. For example, the government tells everyone on the coasts to flee as far inland as possible. Millions may die in the panicked rush to evacuate the coasts but that's better than everyone on the coasts dying because no evacuation was ordered. But what if the government tells everyone to stay put but your all your planning for Armageddon suggests otherwise? What if it's the other way round and you're told to move out when your plans say stay put? What if the recommendations of the Federal authorities and the local authorities are in conflict? Which one will you heed, if either? You are going to have to choose between your faith in the government's ability to protect you from the coming threat and your own assessment of the situation.

Now consider what you'll do if the governments' recommendations concur with your own planning? How closely will you or can you follow their directions when the entire population around you is trying to do the same? These are all factors you'll have to consider.

Obviously the big advantage of even a little advanced warning that civilization is about to crash (and possibly burn) is that you have some time to make some rational decisions. You can act rather than just react. You'll have some time to consider what actions to take in order to survive. What will be crucial is the ability to maintain your calm and prioritize tasks in a rational manner based both on the type of Apocalypse, what everyone else is doing (or not doing as the case may be), and the perceived accuracy of the advanced warning.

Your perception of the accuracy of the advanced warning will color all your actions so it's an issue you should not take lightly. Crazy John downtown telling you Ragnarok starts tomorrow is not the same as NASA telling you there's an asteroid the size of Vermont on a collision course *with* Vermont. Your appraisal of the source's trustworthiness will affect how much time you perceive you have before the civilization goes belly up. Just be careful not to jump to conclusions. Even crackpots are occasionally right and government agencies aren't always completely incompetent.

The big downside to a little advanced warning is it gives you enough time to ponder your doom (and/or the doom of your loved ones) but not enough time to do everything for them and yourself that you want to. You're going to have to cope with hard questions about what to do with your cat, your mom in Peoria, and little sister who's away at college. As you struggle with these tough calls, ask yourself what your loved ones would want you to do. Would they want you to secure your own survival or put yourself at risk in order to try to help them? At the very least, think of the airplane instructions for using the emergency oxygen mask when sitting next to someone who needs help like a child or senior- "secure your own mask first before attempting to help others with theirs" (or something to that effect).

In the event that the advance warning is still not enough time for you to get out of the deadly path of some Apocalyptic juggernaut, at the very least, you have an opportunity to make your peace with God and/or family, and/or yourself. Maybe in the face of eminent death you can find peace and help others do the same.

The Slow-Burn Apocalypse

The Apocalypse is definitely coming and there's no stopping it but it may take a year or so before it arrives. This, in some ways, is the best case scenario and also the worst.

You'll have an enormous survival advantage due to the fact that you should have ample time to stockpile supplies, relocate if need be, coordinate with friends and family, etc. It could also be a chance to form alliances with others to try to ensure your mutual survival.

Faced with the certainty of disaster, humans can still find the ability to persevere and hope. Humanity may find that in facing the extinction of our civilization, we may finally be able to set aside our bickering and work together for the greater good. Humans have a tendency to defy fate and may accomplish extraordinary things in an attempt to avert what is seen as the inevitable. A true Apocalypse is unstoppable but human endeavor holds possible the survival of some and the continuation of the species.

Long-term forewarning can lead to hope but, unfortunately, it can also lead to despair. Despair is the enemy of survival. Despair can lead to mental paralysis, illogical behavior, and sadly, even suicide. When you have lots of time to dwell on the beginning of the end, it's only natural you might feel a little depressed. You must learn to channel that anxiety into positive action. You'll be extra-burdened by the fact that you'll most likely be surrounded by those who are unprepared, or in denial, and you will have to be a source of reason and hope for them as well as for yourself.

The longer people have to ponder the coming of the end, the more time there is for order to start breaking down. The final fall of civilization may be partly precipitated by people's *fear* of the fall of civilization. It may well be you are faced with the prospect of having to survive the Pre-Apocalypse, as well as the Apocalypse and Post-Apocalypse. Keep this in mind as you work on this level of advanced warning.

The good news is that the very fact that you are reading this indicates you are the kind of person who does not give up easily and have no intention of going gently (or otherwise) into "that good night". That determination and persistence will not only keep you from succumbing to hopelessness, it will serve as a source of strength for those around you.

Now you know you need to think of your Apocalyptic planning in terms of proximity. It is not enough to have a cut and run plan for making it through the Apocalypse, you also need to know how to best take advantage of whatever amount of advanced warning you have. Having a lot of time and no plan to exploit it can be almost as dangerous as no time at all.

Chapter 4
ASSESSING YOUR EXISTING SURVIVAL SKILLS

After reading about some of the possible disasters mankind can face, you may be feeling vulnerable and unsure of your ability to survive the "days after". That's only natural. What you may not realize is that you actually do possess some skills that may help you survive and thrive in the dark days to come. You can get a better of idea of what skills you already possess by looking at your life in relevant segments.

Location, Location, Location
Where you live now and where you have lived in the past, both in terms of region and level of urbanization, directly contributes to your survival experience even if you're not aware of it.

Regional Advantages
Of course there will be some generalizations made here but the basics are applicable to a lot of the people in a particular region. If you've spent any appreciable time in a particular region you've adapted to the local climate and have experience coping with the weather extremities of that region. For example, those in the northernmost states understand what it takes to survive a long winter of extreme cold and heavy snow. Those on the Atlantic and Gulf coasts have experience dealing with hurricanes. Southwesterners routinely cope with extremely dry and extremely hot summers and know firsthand what can happen when water runs low. The best prepared for the widest variety of climate extremes are those in the Midwest where they go from triple digit summers of extreme humidity to sub-zero

winters and ice storms to springs filled with flooding, tornadoes, and micro-bursts.

Depending the type of Apocalypse you face, you may find yourself caught completely unprepared for the type of weather conditions that will exist. So if your climate experience is mostly limited to one extreme or another, you would do well to research how to survive in additional climes. Ask yourself if you know what to do to prepare for (and possibly escape from) a tornado, a hurricane, an ice storm, wide-spread flooding, or wild fires. When it comes to preparing for the meteorological conditions that come with the end times, the jack of all trades is in a better position for survival than the specialist.

Urbanization Advantages

The level of urbanization where you have lived most of your life has most likely left you with some special coping skills and experiences.

URBAN: You're emotionally adjusted to living in high density populations and the resulting nuisances such as long lines, limited housing options, heavy traffic, and use of mass transit. You're probably also more attuned to the safety of your surroundings and are wary of suspicious looking individuals. Criminals and gangs are not an unknown menace to you.

SUBURBAN: You may have a stronger sense of community and social identity that leads you to form strong bonds with your neighbors. You may also have enough disposable income that you have experience with things like hunting, fishing, boating, and camping. Your housing situation also more likely lends itself to stockpiling goods and equipment needed to survive what is coming. You definitely know how to drive a car and most likely have at least some college education.

RURAL: You are more self-reliant by necessity. You are used to having to travel long distances to acquire goods and stockpiling comes naturally to you. You're less likely to be dependent on utility companies and more likely to be ready to cope with utility outages. Odds are you own at least one gun and view it as both a tool for acquiring food and as a weapon for defense of your homestead. You may be naturally suspicious of strangers but you're also aware of the importance of a community that helps one another out in hard times.

So now you can see that the environments in which you lived may have already equipped you with some attributes and experience that may come in handy before, during, and after the Apocalypse.

Your Vocation

The job occupations you've held in your life may have bestowed on you certain knowledge and abilities that could come in useful once civilization starts circling the bowl. There are far too many possibilities to try to list in any book so instead you'll have to do a little critical thinking. Here's how to go about it. Start by making a list of every job you've ever held. Now list every responsibility you had at that job. Now, here's where the critical thinking comes in- looking back on the types of possible Apocalypses and the probable results, how might each of your past job responsibilities translate into a survival skill?

For example, let's say you were a lifeguard once which means that at the very least you are a strong swimmer and had CPR training. Both are good survival skills. That one is easy. Now something tougher- you were a customer service associate at a large discount retailer (you handled returns and exchanges). While on the surface it may seem like nothing from this job would help in a post-Apocalyptic world, if you think of it in more general terms, it did give you something. You learned to handle angry and impatient people in an efficient manner. That's a skill that could one day serve you well in a world of food and medicine shortages. Or consider management experience, it may seem like a less important skill than say hunting but being able to manage people and inventories could absolutely make the difference between life and death, not just for yourself but for many others as well.

Your Hobbies

What is meant here are any activities you pursue in your spare time for fun or relaxation. Again, start with a list. What activities do you participate in? What skills and/or knowledge do they require?

Some hobbies' post-Apocalyptic applications, such as hunting, fishing, camping, and martial arts, are readily apparent because they involve general survival skills like living off the land and defending yourself. Other hobbies may have skills that are specific to a certain type of Apocalypse. If you enjoy programming Roombas to do tasks other than vacuum, that can come in handy during a robot uprising. Cross-country skiing may not help much if the ice caps melt but could be invaluable during a new ice age. Collecting hobbies probably won't be as useful unless you're into collecting things like weapons, ammunition, MRE's, Geiger counters, and/or Hazmat suits.

Assessing the survival values of your hobbies is no different than assessing your work experience. Look at what qualities and knowledge your hobbies take and compare them against the possible Apocalypse scenarios. You may well find your hobbies are more useful than you initially thought.

Post-Apocalyptic Survival and Success Assessment (PASSA)
Use the tables on the following pages to get a clearer idea of your skills and skill levels to help you create a personal plan of action for developing the attributes of a successful Post-Apocalyptic resident.

TRANSPORTATION:

Give yourself 1 point for every mode of transportation you have had experience operating. Give yourself an additional point for every mode of transportation you consider yourself an expert at or are licensed to operate. Then add up the totals from each mode for your Post-Apocalyptic Transportation Preparedness Score.

Mode	Type	Type	Type	Type	Type	Type	Mode Total
Wheeled	Golf/Utility Cart	Automobile	Tractor Trailer	Motorcycle	ATV	Light Rail	
Watercraft	Canoe/Row boat	Jet Ski	Motorboat	Air Boat	Sail Boat	Steam Boat	
Aircraft	Jet Pack	Hang Glider	Gyrocopter	Helicopter	Small Prop Plane	Jet Plain	
Other	Hovercraft	Treaded	Snow Mobile	Snow Skis	Dog Sled	Horse/Camel	

Post-Apocalyptic Transportation Preparedness Score _____ of 48 points

HANDS-ON SKILLS:

Give yourself 1 point for every skill you have some experience with. Give yourself an additional point for every skill you consider yourself an expert at or for which you have professional certification or credentials. Then add up the totals from each mode for your Post-Apocalyptic Hands-On Preparedness Score.

Skill	Type	Type	Type	Type	Type	Type	Skill Total
Engine Repair	Electric	Small Gas	Car	Semi	Motorcycle	Steam	
Building	Carpentry	Welding	Plumbing	Electricity	Masonry	Insulation	
Farming	Plowing	Planting	Harvesting	Irrigation	Storage	Meat Preservation	
Livestock	Breeding	Feeding	Veterinary Medicine	Birthing	Slaughtering	Snow Removal	
Other	Demolitions	Excavation	Logging	Paving	Sewage		
						Post-Apocalyptic Hands-On Preparedness Score	___ of 58 points

MANAGEMENT SKILLS:

Give yourself 1 point for every management skill you have some experience with. Give yourself an additional point for every skill you consider yourself an expert at or for which you have professional certification or credentials. Then add up the totals from each mode for your Post-Apocalyptic Management Preparedness Score.

Skill	Type	Type	Type	Type	Type	Type	Skill Total
People-Blue Collar	10 or fewer	50 or fewer	100 or fewer	500 or fewer	1000 or fewer	10k+	
People-White Collar	10 or fewer	50 or fewer	100 or fewer	500 or fewer	1000 or fewer	10k+	
Retail Inventory	1 location	District Mgr.	State Mgr.	Regional Mgr.	Executive		
Restaurant/ Grocery Inventory	1 location	District Mgr.	State Mgr.	Regional Mgr.	Executive		
Construction Inventory	Residential	Retail	Commercial	Government			
Chemical Inventory	Pharmaceutical	Industrial					
					Post-Apocalyptic Management Preparedness Score	____ of 56 points	

MEDICAL SKILLS:

Give yourself 1 point for every skill you have some experience with. Give yourself an additional point for every skill you consider yourself an expert at or for which you have professional certification or credentials. Then add up the totals from each mode for your Post-Apocalyptic Medical Preparedness Score.

Skill	Type	Type	Type	Type	Type	Type	Skill Total
First Aid Training	Scouting	Life Guard	Civil Servant	Childcare	Military		
Are You A... (2 pts each)	EMT	Paramedic	Street Medic	Flight Medic	Wilderness EMT		
Are You A... (2 pts each)	LPN	RN	Office Nurse	Hospital Nurse	Occupational Health Nurse	Surgical Nurse	
Are You A... (2 pts each)	MD	Surgeon	Pharmacist	Anesthesiologist	Medical Researcher	Psychiatrist	
Are You A Combat Experienced... (2 pts each)	Military Medic	Field Surgeon	Field Nurse				
						Post-Apocalyptic Medical Preparedness Score	___ of 50 points

ATHLETIC SKILLS:

Give yourself 1 point for every skill you have some experience with. Give yourself an additional point for every skill you consider yourself an expert at or for which you have collegiate, semi-pro, professional experience or certification. Then add up the totals from each mode for your Post-Apocalyptic Athletics Preparedness Score.

Skill	Type	Type	Type	Type	Type	Skill Total
Long Distance / Racing	Marathon	Cycling	Swimming	Snow Skiing	Rowing	
Other Athletic Activities	Parkour	Rock Climbing	Repelling	Spelunking	Scuba	
Post-Apocalyptic Athletics Preparedness Score						____ of 20 points

COMBAT:
Give yourself 1 point for every area you have had experience. Give yourself an additional point for each area you consider yourself an expert at or have some military or law enforcement certification or competed in a pro or semi-pro circuit. Then add up the totals from each mode for your Post-Apocalyptic Combat Preparedness Score.

Skill	Type	Type	Type	Type	Type	Type	Type Total
Unarmed	Boxing	MMA	Traditional Martial Art	Military Training	Law Enforcement Training		
Armed, Melee	Knives	Swords or Long Blades	Sticks or Batons	Staff	Other	Other	
Firearms	Handguns	Hunting Rifles	Military Rifles	Fully Auto Firearms	Grenade Launchers	Black Powder	
Other	Archery	Javelins	Throwing Blades	Hand Grenades	Mines/IEDs	Booby Traps	
						Post-Apocalyptic Combat Preparedness Score	___ of 46 points

WILDERNESS SKILLS:

Give yourself 1 point for every skill you have some experience with. Give yourself an additional point for every skill you consider yourself an expert at or that you have received formal training in. Then add up the totals from each mode for your Post-Apocalyptic Wilderness Preparedness Score.

Skill	Type	Type	Type	Type	Type	Type	Skill Total
Food Acquisition	Fishing	Hunting	Tracking	Plant Identification	Food Preservation	Safe Drinking Water Identification	
Specialized	Arctic Survival	Jungle Survival	Desert Survival	Sea Survival			
Shelter	Modern Camping	Wilderness Camping	Mountain Camping				
Escape And Evasion (6 points)	SERE Graduate					Post-Apocalyptic Wilderness Preparedness Score	____ of 32 points

____ Transportation score

____ Hands-On score

____ Management score

____ Medical score

____ Athletic score

____ Combat score

____ Wilderness score

Total PASSA points possible = 310

_____ Your PASSA score

Interpreting Your Post-Apocalyptic Survival and Success Assessment

Remember, the PASSA is not a pass or fail test. It's not a test at all. It is a generalized inventory of the skills and knowledge you possess that may help you both survive the Apocalypse and maybe even thrive in the aftermath. It is by no means comprehensive but it should be sufficient in helping you determine your level of general readiness and can help you identify whole areas or specific skills in which you may want to expand your knowledge and experience.

If your PASSA score is less than you might have expected or less than you feel is ideal, keep in mind, it is a generalized inventory of skill that no one can get 100% on. In fact, if you got 50% or more, you're probably well on your way to making it in a Post-Apocalyptic world. No matter what your score, you now have a huge advantage in that you now know what you don't know and can do something about it.

Chapter 5
CIVILIZATION AFTER THE FALL OF CIVILIZATION

Unless the entire human race goes extinct, the one thing you can count on is that no matter how hard civilization has fallen, people will immediately begin to organize. It's what humans do. They will begin to band together for common purposes and try to begin establishing some social order. It may take awhile before any real order becomes evident, however.

Naturally, the aftermath of an Apocalyptic event is going be pretty chaotic. Exactly how chaotic things will be on the day after Doomsday is purely speculative. The chaos factor will be dependent on the type of Apocalypse, your geographic location, how much advanced warning there was, and, of course, pure dumb luck.

The level of chaos can be measured in two ways:
1. Personal Chaos Level
2. Surrounding Chaos Level

Your Personal Chaos Level represents the immediate impact the Apocalypse had on you and your immediate family and how much loss was mitigated by your survival preparations. The Surrounding Chaos Level represents how much social and natural upheaval has happened in you locale. Due to luck or preparation, you may have escaped the Apocalypse relatively unscathed but your city has been laid to waste and there's been a complete breakdown in social order. Things could go the opposite way, your city or county makes it through the Apocalypse with only minor damage and casualties but part of the damage was your house and/or some of the casualties were your family members.

Meditate on that for a minute. Something should start becoming clear. No man is an island. No matter how much preparation you do, your fate is still going to largely tied to the community around you. Even if you live in the middle of nowhere, the events of the Apocalypse could turn your locale into a gigantic refugee camp. It's understandable to resent having your fate tied to all the people around you who fiddle while Rome burns. Those who behave responsibly always get leaned on by the irresponsible. That's human nature. Naturally, the Apocalypse will quickly weed out a lot of those who can't or won't ready themselves for what's to come but many will make it through anyway.

The best way to deal with those people is to start helping them help themselves before the end comes. Yes, you have, or are in the process of, taking all the possible steps you can to ensure your long-term survival and success but your work shouldn't stop at your property line. You owe it to yourself and your loved ones to get involved in your community's emergency preparedness. There are numerous government and private sector programs devoted to educating civilians on disaster response and planning. The more your neighbors are prepared, the less likely they are to expect you to carry them through the hard times to come. If it helps, you can also consider it in this self-serving way- the more you participate in community planning and preparedness, the better equipped the community will be to come to *your* rescue should you draw the short straw on the day it all falls apart. Helping your community today is helping yourself tomorrow.

SOCIAL POCKETS OF THE POST-APOCALYPSE

The social structures that emerge in the days after won't be that much different than they've been in some of mankind's more uncivilized eras. People will band together to meet their basic needs of food, shelter, and safety. There will also be those who use the situation to profit either through trade or through force. Below are some of the social clusterings you will likely encounter.

Settlements

This would be any semi-permanent attempts at building a community voluntarily. The people there are there by choice, not force and have a say in communal issues. The government of the community will likely vary from democratic to communist but it will not be maintained through threat of violence. There will however most likely be some specific rules which everyone has agreed to live by and the punishment for violating those rules may be severe.

The settlement is an attempt to establish order and to produce as a group what cannot be produced as an individual- security, services, and goods. Resources necessary for survival may also be pooled and evenly distributed. Settlements will be the beginning attempts to rebuild what has been lost.

Trading Outposts

Trading outposts will be privately run affairs that will most likely try to maintain a completely neutral stance. The various groups roaming the Apocalypse will conform to the conditions dictated by the trading outpost because the outpost will be the one place where you can find just about anything you need. Banishment from an outpost for not respecting its position as neutral ground could be a devastating blow for a post-Apocalyptic survivor.

The trading outpost will be run as a business and maintain its own small private army for the purpose of maintaining order and enforcing rules. The trading outpost thrives on a sense of order and security. The outpost may also enforce rules regarding trades and act as the final arbiter in dispute resolution.

Over time, it is possible that a settlement may grow up around the trading post that provides services to those that come to trade such as medical, food, fuel, shelter, and sex. Over time, the trading outpost itself may be absorbed into the greater community that has sprung up around it. The outpost may also find itself coerced or pressured into becoming the subject of a stronger military force which taxes it or determines who may trade with the outpost. Whatever the case, the trading outpost and commerce it spawns will play a vital role in rebuilding the civilization after the Apocalypse.

Bandit Enclaves

Naturally, there will be those who see the post-Apocalypse as a prime opportunity to prey upon the weak and unwary. They will form bands devoted to taking what they want from whomever they want. Most likely they will establish a permanent base of operations near their primary hunting grounds. Even bandits may find it necessary to establish relationships with travelling traders in order to obtain things they can't steal from others and as a way of pawning things they have pilfered that are of no use to them.

Where bandits hole up will vary depending on the terrain, locale, etc. It would likely lay not too far off one of the more well travelled roads or waterways, probably camouflaged to some degree. A known bandit lair should be approached with extreme caution. Bandits will be paranoid about their security as they will fear being attacked by rivals, authorities, and vengeful victims. It should be assumed that any bandit hideout will be guarded, inside and out, by booby-traps, primitive alarms, and possibly trained guard dogs. It should also be assumed that they are heavily armed and likely to shoot first and ask questions later.

Warlord Encampments

In the chaotic days that follow the Apocalypse there will be those that will seek to secure supplies and restore a semblance of order through the use of force. They are not offering their services and protection to a population, they are imposing their will through implied, or direct use, of violence on a population. The types of people who attempt this could include:

- Religious crusaders
- Officials from the former civilian government
- Former soldiers
- Criminal bosses

A warlord's motives will run the gamut from cruel and exploitative to benign dictatorship. Either way, understand this, they not going to ask for permission or put anything up to a vote. An encounter with a warlord's forces could end with you conscripted, enslaved, robbed (taxed), raped, and/or dead.

Still, warlords present opportunities for non-combatants. Armies need to be supplied. At the very least, there will be need for cooks, doctors, and armorers of one sort or another. Depending on the post-Apocalyptic conditions, there may also be need for animal handlers, mechanics, sex workers, cobblers, spies, messengers, and more.

Overall, it is best to avoid warlords and their armies unless you are seeking specific work or if seeking protection from a rival warlord. If you do deliberately choose to engage with a warlord or his/her representatives, do not expect what you would consider fair treatment. Unless you possess some particularly valuable skills or knowledge, you'll probably be viewed as expendable and grousing will be probably be met with pain or death. If you choose to sign up as a soldier under a warlord keep in mind that you may be expected to do things that would have violated international law back before the Apocalypse. The killing of civilians, women, and children may be commonplace. The same goes for rape and torture. Be sure you know what you're getting into before you volunteer because refusing to obey orders will probably be a capital offense.

Refugee Camps
Should you find yourself a refugee from nature or man or whatever, you may want to think twice before moving into a refugee camp, whether it's just makeshift or set up by some governmental or religious organization. Just consider for a moment the conditions faced by hurricane Katrina refugees in the Superdome or the plight of refugees in Darfur.

There are a number of reasons why you may be better going it alone or in a very small group.

1. *Sanitation-* Refugee camps are notorious for having horrendous sanitary conditions. Improper waste disposal and unclean drinking water can lead to parasitic infections, dysentery, cholera, typhus fever, typhoid, schistosomiasis and trachoma.

2. *Lack of Internal Security-* Refugee camps may have formal or informal security or no security at all. Some refugees may form gangs that run prostitution and protection rackets. You may find your possessions (including your pets and children), if left unguarded, targeted by thieves. If you have something that is very scarce and of particular value, such as food or medicine, you may find it taken by force by your fellow refugees or even the so-called authorities who are supposed to be protecting you.

3. *Target Potential-* Sadly, refugee camps have a big bullseye on them. Bandits, slavers, and other human preda-

tors may prey on refugees who stray too far from the camp in search of food, water, and firewood. Warlords may view camps as a source of slaves or "recruits". The most dangerous potential risk a refugee camp holds is that some power, be it government or some other faction, see the camp as a competitor for resources or as breeding ground for disease or dissent that needs to be eliminated or contained. What started as a refugee camp may morph into a concentration or prison camp or abattoir. Human history has been frequently been cruel to refugees.

At the very least, before joining a refugee camp, observe the camp from a distance to see who is coming and going from the camp. If it seems safe, stash your valuables and try approaching the camp to gather more intel. Try to determine:

- Who is in charge?
- What sanitation conditions exist?
- Is there any sense of law and order?
- Do the refugees feel hopeful or hopeless?
- What are the rumors of the camp's future?
- Is there any attempt at an organized social order?
- Are refugees free to come and go?
- How scarce are food, water, and medicine?

While there is something to the truism "safety in numbers", it may be safer to stick to smaller numbers. A small group has a better chance of passing through unnoticed. Even if noticed by hostiles, a smaller group may be passed over in favor of the larger, more potentially lucrative group. A small group means fewer people to divide resources among and the ability to exercise more control over sanitation conditions.

Ruins

The ruins of the civilization that was may harbor great dangers, be great sources of goods, or both. Obviously, the type of Apocalypse experienced will determine exactly how many ruins are left to begin with. Ruins may be more plentiful than people or practically non-existent. Whether ruins are a good source of supplies will depend on how much Apocalyptic notice was had and how long the Apocalypse was drawn out.

Whatever the case, the one thing you should expect to find in ruins is death. The corpses of those who perished in the Apocalypse will likely litter the landscape. Even in municipalities that were evacuated, there will have been those who refused to leave or who were incapable of leaving. Before entering, steel yourself for some gruesome and heart-wrenching sights.

Ruins will generally come in one of two forms:

1.) *Intact and Abandoned-* These are ruins that are structurally sound but have been abandoned. Intact does not necessarily mean safe. They may be harboring dangers like radiation, toxins, wild animals, infected persons, rogue technology, and/or gangs.

2.) *Fully or Partially Destroyed-* These are ruins whose physical integrity was compromised by the events of the Apocalypse. They may be burned or structurally unsound or collapsed. One should enter these ruins with extreme caution. The potential for survival necessities must be carefully weighed against the possibility of death or injury amongst the unstable structures. In addition to their structural dangers, they may also hide the same dangers you face in intact ruins. Proceed at your own risk.

Still, with all the risks ruins present, they can be invaluable source of necessities like medicine, clothing, fuel, ammunition, and barter goods.

Military Installations

Again, depending on the type of Apocalypse that occurred, military installations may have weathered the storm better than most other places. Even installations that were not generally built to withstand any kind of attack, there will be some fortified buildings and bunkers that may be quite intact and sheltering survivors.

A military installation can be a jackpot for survivors. Typically one could expect to find rugged clothing, preserved food, general survival and camping gear, weapons, ammunition, vehicles, fuel, medicine, maps, communication devices, and so on. The odds are however that you are not the only person aware of this potential.

If the installation survived relatively intact, it is likely there will be some soldiers still present. How friendly they'll be to other survivors is anybody's guess. For this reason, approach carefully. Don't try to sneak up on it, that may be seen as hostile and get you shot. Approach openly in the daylight with weapons stowed and hands clearly visible. If you're confronted and told to leave, don't argue, just turn and leave quietly. You don't want to piss off people with easy access to automatic weapons.

If soldiers allow you to approach, don't expect them to be willing to give away supplies or to offer you shelter. If they do offer you anything, carefully examine the strings attached to the offer to make sure it is worth your while. Whatever noble traditions and intentions the armed forces may have once strived for may not have survived the fall of civilization.

In the event there are no soldiers, it is likely the base will have already been ransacked long before your arrival. Still, looters may have left behind a treasure trove of, well, loot. Even if main storage areas and supply depots have been raided, personal living quarters may have been altogether ignored.

One should also consider the possibility that the installation has been turned into a permanent settlement by the soldiers and their families or that some other group has taken up permanent residence there. If this appears to be the case, approach with the utmost caution because you have no idea how they will view outsiders and assume they will definitely have the capacity to shoot first and ask questions later.

CAREERS OF THE POST-APOCALYPSE

In some ways, if you manage to survive the Apocalypse, not much will have changed. You will still need to acquire and maintain sources of food, water, medicine, clothing, and shelter. The ways of getting what you need are:

- *Find It*- claiming abandoned assets in ruins or acquiring them from nature
- *Make It*- use you skills and ingenuity to create what is needed
- *Steal It*- find someone who has what you need and take it through force, fraud, or stealth
- *Barter For It*- trade goods and/or services for the things you need

Most of your post-Apocalyptic career paths will revolve around one or more of the above four methods for obtaining what you need to survive today and thrive tomorrow. Let's take a look at some of the possibilities.

Scavenger

To one degree or another, everyone who makes it to the day after Doomsday will end up doing some scavenging out of necessity. Some might feel some hesitation at first because what today qualifies as survival scavenging yesterday was viewed as opportunistic looting. You'll get over that sense of hesitance quick. If not, you'll probably die.

While everyone will be doing it to some extent, some folks will choose to take up scavenging as their full-time occupation. The smart survivor will quickly assess what the most valuable and hard to obtain commodities are and scour the wastelands for sources. The professional scavenger will have to find the safest and most lucrative way to trade his found booty for the things he wants and needs.

One option is to sell to a single source such as travelling merchant, a warlord, or a contact within a trading outpost. This method is the simplest and minimizes the possibility of getting caught up in the hostilities between various factions. The downside is that you make less selling to a middleman than selling directly to the end user.

The other choice is to act as both scavenger and merchant, going from location to location hawking your wares or holding auctions at trading outposts. While you've cut out the middleman, you have to carefully navigate the politics of the wasteland and you're more likely to be targeted by thieves.

Either way, the life of a scavenger can be a dangerous one. To be truly successful, one has to be willing to go in search of goods in places most others are not. A good may be valuable because it is mainly found in a place fraught with contamination, treacherous landscape, dangerous wildlife, cutthroats, hostile technology, or all of the aforementioned hazards combined. If a scavenger wants to have a long career he or she will need to become an expert in evading or overcoming the dangers the Apocalypse has left in its wake.

Travelling Merchant

Goods of different types naturally tend to accumulate is different localities and there is a profit to be made by the person willing to ferry those goods around to where they are in demand. That person is the travelling merchant.

Becoming a travelling merchant requires considerable logistical planning. Anyone thinking of taking up this trade will want to begin by evaluating these issues:

1.) *What Goods Should You Trade In?* This one is not as simple as you might first think. Do you go for high volumes in inexpensive, common, easy to obtain commodities or do you go for small volumes of the rare and expensive? Are there any items you won't traffic for moral reasons? Will the goods you deal in effect your relations with various factions?

2.) *Who Will You Trade With?* Will you trade with anyone for anything or will you refuse to do business with some? If you try to trade with all, will you be able to convince all parties of your neutrality? If you choose to exclude some parties from trading, will it put you at risk? Will you be willing to exclude some goods from your inventory in order to appease the morality of a trading partner?

3.) *What Is The Standard Unit Of Trade?* Paper money will be worthless after the fall of the civilization that created it so, what will be the unit of exchange? Some might assume a default to gold but gold's value will be determined by the conditions people are living in. People starving can't eat gold; people dying of radiation sickness won't have much need of gold either. So the issue becomes one of identifying if conditions are such that some form of currency can be instituted or if trade will be a true barter system. Humans adopt currency for good reasons but before you begin to accept currency from one party in exchange for your goods, you'll have to be sure that that currency will be honored by your other trading partners. Also be aware that an invading force might impose its own currency on your trading partners making any of the old currency you possess worthless. If you choose to stick to straight barter, how will you determine what is a fair trade?

4.) *How Will You Transport Goods?* What sort of terrain will your trade routes cover? Will you arrange for all your own transportation or will you charter some parts? How will the types of transportation available to you affect the types of goods you can traffic in? How realistically can you fuel and maintain your proposed mode of transportation for the foreseeable future?

5.) *What Kind Of Security Will You Need?* The wastelands of the post-Apocalypse might be dangerous for a person to traverse. How much more dangerous will travel be when the traveler is carry goods of value to others? Lots of goods of value to others? What will you need to protect you and your goods from? Will you need to hire guards to protect you from humans and animals and other hostiles? Will you need protection from environmental conditions like biological contamination, ash storms, blizzards, or sulfuric gases? How much trade will you need to do in order to balance out the cost of security? How will you deal with demands of protection payments from various authorities and rogues?

So you see that trying to run a business after the fall of civilization will still entail a good deal of strategic planning and a revised version of the same old bureaucratic wrangling, public relations, and asset management- only slightly more dangerous.

Service Provider
Even after the fall of civilization there will be a need for various services. Certainly, those skill sets deemed "blue collar" today will be in demand the most: plumbers, electricians, carpenters, welders, mechanics, farmers, etc. There will most likely be a survivors' emphasis on rebuilding what was or reinforcing/fortifying what is left. There will also be a need for those who can make sure whatever modes of transportation are left can run on what fuels are available.

That doesn't mean those with more "white collar" jobs are out of luck. Medical professions of all stripes will still be in demand, maybe even more so than before. Those with strong management skills and leadership ability will also be needed. Chemists, architects, engineers, and accountants may also find their skills in demand as survivors of the Apocalypse gather in larger numbers, be it in settlements or armies.

There are some professionals that may not be in huge demand today that might be in bigger demand due to post-Apocalyptic conditions. These could include: gunsmiths, bowyers/fletchers, blacksmiths, mid-wives, robotics programmers, alternative energy experts, radiation experts, animal trainers, trackers, and hunters.

What will remain to be seen, regardless of what skills you possess, is whether you end up having any choice in who employs your services. Survival after Doomsday may depend on you performing services for those you abhor.

Bandit

Here bandit refers to anyone whose subsistence is based on taking what they want from others through force and threat of violence. Being a bandit or highwayman is definitely a risky business. You will, no doubt, have the element of surprise on your side but not all your victims will passively give up their belongings and those upon whom you most frequently prey will have a tendency to put a bounty on your head. Still, banditry will hold a definite appeal to a certain class of people that view it as a romanticized path to freedom from society, a way to take vengeance on society, or as a means to a socio-political end.

In a modern Western civilization context, bandits are viewed as villainous and amoral. The Apocalypse however, may end up redefining the social standing of the lowly bandit. That social standing may be affected by who the bandit preys upon and what he does with the spoils from his crimes. In the days after the fall of civilization, thieves and robbers may be subject to a degree of moral relativism.

Without question, the bandit who preys upon the weak and unsuspecting will be little more than a sociopathic opportunist. Other bandits may choose to prey upon those they see as deserving such as warlords, military/government enclaves, slavers, other bandits, and anyone else they think can afford to part with some of their goods. The local populace may forgive the bandit their transgressions if he or she is targeting those the average people consider to be a menace or political adversary. That forgiveness may even evolve into admiration if the bandit shares his spoils with the common people ala Robin Hood.

The degree to which banditry is a viable full-time profession will largely be dependent on the size of the target prey and how well armed they are. If there's no authority around to outlaw guns, then outlaws will not be the only ones with guns (or whatever weapons are prominent). Finally, a bandit will have to decide whether to work alone or to seek out partners in crime. Whether true partners are found or henchmen are hired, the bandit would do well to keep in mind that there may not be much honor among thieves.

Warlord

There will be those who see the Apocalypse as their chance to carve out a large share of whatever pie remains through military force. Warlord here, does not mean the military leader of a settlement, it means someone whose primary goal is to subject others to his rule through military force.

Warlords may arise quickly after the Apocalypse from what remains of the ranks of the former military establishment or from pre-Apocalyptic gangs or criminal organizations. There is also the possibility that a religious leader may try to wage a crusade.

Trying to rise up as a warlord is a hazardous proposal as there will be plenty of contenders willing to kill to reach the same position. Warlords will also be thoroughly hated by those they conquer and possibly by those they employ if they don't pay well or mistreat their troops and retinues. Remember Julius Caesar's fate?

Warlords may use a number of justifications for their actions such as:

- Attempting to restore order in the wake of the Apocalypse
- Establishing a new kingdom in the name of some God
- Purging of ethnic or religious scapegoats
- Re-establishing pre-Apocalyptic government

And of course there will simply be those who seek to rape, pillage, and plunder for their own personal gratification.

While it may seem hard to see anything positive in the concept of post-Apocalyptic warlords, the conditions may necessitate a strong leader who will do what is necessary to unite the remnants of humanity before any kind of stability and self-governance can take hold.

Lone Wanderer

Romanticize this role at your own risk. The reality is there is safety in numbers and anyone who tries to go it alone for any extended period of time will likely not last long. Do not expect to be trusted by anyone or welcome anywhere. Even if you set out to be some Lone Ranger of the wastelands, people will view with suspicion anyone who chooses to remain an outsider to all groups. You may have heroic intentions but they may not be viewed as such even by the people they're intended to help.

This is just a partial list of the possible occupations that await you after the world as we know it comes to an end. Choose you new profession carefully and be prepared to change it at a moment's notice should the need arise.

POLITICS OF THE POST-APOCALYPSE

You might think everyone will view the collapse of civilization as a bad thing but that will hardly be the case. There will be many who see the reduced population and collapse of the social order as an opportunity to create a new and different society based on such concepts as theology, communism, libertarianism, agrarianism, tribalism, etc. In some instances, these would-be creators of a new social order will try to use logic and/or emotional appeals to convince you to follow them. In other instances, they may simply resort to threats and violence.

Some may plainly claim to desire the re-establishment of the nation as it was. To many that will sound ideal, but you should follow these people cautiously because their idea of how things were or should have been may differ drastically from yours. Should elements of the former government try to re-assert their authority, you may find the remnants of the military in conflict with the civilian bureaucrats. That may force you to choose to side with the military, which would be stronger at re-establishing physical security or side with the civil servants who would be better at re-establishing some form of democracy and social programs.

Ultimately, as humans organize and try to re-establish some sense of order, political conflicts will emerge. Even if you consider yourself apolitical now, you should not count on being able to maintain such a position after the Apocalypse. Others will seek to draw you and your loved ones into their conflicts whether you like it or not. This will be especially true if you end up in a refugee camp. Political conflict could undoubtedly turn violent if resources such as food, water, medicine, and shelter are in short supply.

The makeup of the post-Apocalyptic political landscape will be shaped by many factors. One factor will be who makes up the largest portion of survivors based on such things as race, religion, geography, etc. The type of Apocalypse will also affect the direction politics takes. Survivors' perceptions of how things should be run will be greatly influenced by whether or not the Apocalypse is seen as having been man-made or natural in origin. The Apocalypse's impact on resources such as food and water will also impact people's political leanings. Lastly, the extent of threats that need to be actively guarded against (such as wild animals, zombies, mutants, cyborgs, cannibals, etc.), will also largely shape the political order survivors favor.

What this means for you is that you need to really search your beliefs and convictions so that you know what principles you are willing to fight for and where you are willing to make compromises. Will you lead, follow, or go it alone? Just as the conditions of the post-Apocalypse will shape politics, so will you as an individual. The only question is, how active of a participant will you be?

Chapter 6
Fight Or Die

For some, the Apocalypse will reveal in them a strength and nobility in them they never knew they possessed. For others, however, the collapse of order will release the monster that heretofore was only kept in check by fear of punishment or loss of social standing. Desperate times will also lead desperate people to commit acts they previously would never even have considered. If your fellow man was not threat enough, nature may be out to prey on you as well. It should be coming clear that if you want to survive the wasteland, pacifism is not a choice unless you are an absolute master of camouflage, armor, running, hiding, fast-talking, and bribery. If that's not you, then you had better be prepared to fight.

Indentifying Threats

Here are some of the possible foes you may encounter after the Apocalypse:

1.) *Wildlife-* What sort of wildlife you'll encounter will largely be determined by the type of Apocalypse experienced. The majority of wildlife may have been wiped out or the majority of it might be driven into your area in high concentrations. Bears and big cats could suddenly appear in areas they had long been banished from by humans. If there has been extensive flooding, aquatic predators may be more of a threat than ever before.

   One threat you will almost certainly face will be dogs. There are approximately 74 million dogs in the United States alone. As it is, according to the Centers For Disease Control (CDC), over 350,000 people are treated in emergency rooms each year for dog bites. The CDC numbers also showed an average of 17 dog-related deaths a year during the 1980's and 1990's and since then the number has risen to a peak of 33 deaths in 2007. If that's how dangerous today's domesticated dogs are, how dangerous will they be when civilization collapses? Do not underestimate how quickly once-domesticated dogs turn feral. Hunger could easily drive them to view humans as food. The ruins of suburbia will likely see large numbers of dog packs that are fast moving and unafraid of their former masters.

There is also the possibility that animals from zoos and nature sanctuaries escaped, or were purposely released, during or after the Apocalypse. Consider for a moment the terrifying possibility of lions and tigers roaming across the landscape. With any animals, conditions arising from the Apocalypse, such as starvation or disease, could lead them to be more aggressive towards humans than they would be otherwise.

2.) *Amoral Humans-* This means people who are deliberately seeking to injure or kill others simply because they want to or because they can profit from it. There will be the plain old sociopaths who seek to rape, maim, and murder for no other reason than it amuses them. There will also be those who seek to take from anyone they can and have no compunctions about killing to get what they want. Slavery, particularly sex slavery, will also raise its ugly head shortly after the collapse of law and order. You may not be appealing to a slaver but those under your protection might be. If there are warlords around, you may also encounter press gangs looking for people to force into military service.

3.) *Desperate Humans-* Some humans, desperate to stay alive, may resort to violence. They may feel they are justified in taking from you because you have more than they, thanks to your pre-Apocalypse preparations. It is also not unlikely that faced with the starvation of their children or yours, they will choose to take from yours to feed their own, if they have the means to. Unprepared survivors could pose a major risk and while you may want to show them compassion, you should use extreme caution when dealing with them.

4.) *The Diseased and Demented-* Maybe the saddest danger you will encounter will come from those the Apocalypse has left irrationally violent and possibly contagious due to disease, biological/chemical exposure, or simply trauma-induced insanity. These poor souls will be of all ages, genders, and creeds. You will not be able to reason with them and they will likely be beyond your ability to aid them. Do not let your compassion undermine your assessment of the danger they may represent.

5.) *The Contagious-* In the event that the Apocalypse was caused by a contagion or that contagions are one of the by-products of the Apocalypse, one needs to consider the lengths you're willing to go to keep the contagious, or possibly contagious, at bay. Again, it is not that you should suppress all compassion for others but you will have to weigh your compassion with the need to protect you and those in your party.

6.) *Fanatics-* When disaster strikes, people want someone to blame (anyone but themselves). The Apocalypse is the biggest disaster imaginable and in some survivors it may unleash previously suppressed bigotries and prejudices. Members of certain ethnic, social, political, or religious persuasions may find themselves and the people they associate with targeted for retribution, consisting of everything from rape to torture and even murder. In the days after the collapse of the civilization that spawned the world's greatest ethnic and religious melting pot, ethnic cleansing and religious jihad/crusading may once again become a grim reality.

7.) *Press Gangs-* Press gangs are sent out by would-be warlords to forcibly conscript soldiers for their armies.

8.) *Apocalypse-Dependent Hostiles-* Any hostiles that may be unique to a particular type of Apocalypse such as robots, aliens, demons, mutants, etc.

Tools Of The Trade

Once you've come to accept the probability that you may have to resort to violence in order to survive in the post-Apocalyptic landscape, you're going to have to give some serious thought to exactly what you will use to defend yourself, your loved ones, and your property.

There are far too many weapons to consider in depth here but a brief general overview of the major options is in order.

1.) *Martial Arts-* A mastery of an unarmed martial art provides an indispensible foundation for your self-defense efforts. It's been endlessly debated which art is most effective and some styles are more popular at any one point in time than others. If you are looking for an art, here are a few brief guidelines for choosing a style:
   a. Does the style fit your body type and any physical limitations you have?

    b. *Are you physically capable of performing major elements of the style such as high kicks, low stances, throws, rolls/falls, etc?*
    c. *Can you get instruction for a price you can afford and at a time and location you can make on a regular basis?*
    d. *Are there books and videos available that can augment your training?*
    e. *Is the art adaptable to different styles of dress? In other words, will the art be practical regardless as to whether you are half-naked or wearing layers of cold-weather clothing or a chemical/radiation suit?*

    Whatever style you choose, practice, practice, practice. Self-defense moves aren't of much use if they're not burned into muscle-memory and come to you reflexively. And if it all possible, train with a variety of live partners and work your way up to full contact. If you train to always pull your strikes, you'll likely do the same in a real fight because that's how you've conditioned yourself. You fight the way you train so find a way to train the way you want to be able to fight.

2.) *Long Guns*- Rifles and, to a lesser extent shotguns, allow you to take down game and hostile targets from further away than any other handheld weapon. They come in a wide variety from single shot bolt-action to fully-auto and small caliber .22 to the .700 Nitro Express elephant stopper. Rifles and shotguns are very common guns in America and the standard ammunitions such as .22, .223, .30-30, and .30-06 are fairly easy to come by in discount retailers and sporting goods stores. There are also a variety of rifles and pistols that can shoot both .410 shotgun shells and .45 pistol cartridges. If you're unsure what to get, consult an expert in a gun organization or a reputable gun dealer and try different kinds to find one that fits your budget and your physical build. The purchasing of firearms is not an area you should skimp on research. Making uninformed decisions when it comes to guns could be just as bad as having no guns at all. The downside to rifles is that they are generally not the best choice in close quarters, the exception possibly being a sawed-off shotgun.

3.) *Handguns-* Handguns are best suited for medium and close range and depending on the caliber can have considerable stopping power. The most common calibers would be 9mm, .22, and .38- none of which should be too difficult to come by. Some handguns can even use more than one caliber of bullet, a good trait if you're having to scavenge for ammo. As with long guns, seek out professional advice on choosing a gun and try many styles and calibers before making a purchase. Finally, training in defensive handgun use is a must! It is not an option. Many gun organizations offer training and certification. Seek them out.

4.) *Archery-* Archery has been around almost as long as modern man. Given the choice between a firearm and a bow, firearms are the hands down winner but that doesn't mean the bow can't be a vital addition to your arsenal. Consider the two major advantages of archery: reusable ammo and quietness. If you can't buy a firearm due to being a convicted felon or draconian gun laws where you live, a good bow or crossbow could serve you well until after the Apocalypse (when breaking gun laws will be the least of your worries). Bows come in a wide variety from short to long to traditional to compound. If you opt for archery as your primary ranged weapon, you had better practice like crazy because as any experienced bow hunter will tell you, it's hard enough hitting a stationary animal when you're calm much less hitting a radioactive maniac who is charging at you with a machete. Lastly, you had also better learn to fletch arrows as there may not be a Bass Pro Shop handy when you run out of arrows for your bow or bolts for your crossbow.

5.) *Throwing Weapons-* It is one thing to have a weapon that, in a pinch, can be thrown but it's quite something else to consider thrown weapons as the primary component of your arsenal. The number you'll be able to carry will be far more limited than bullets or arrows. The range of thrown weapons can't begin to compete with a bow much less a gun. Without a very forceful and accurate throw, your weapons will likely not be lethal. Sure you could add poison but you're not likely to have access to super-fast acting toxins, as a general rule. There's nothing wrong with carrying a dual purpose melee/throwing weapon or a few dedicated throwing weapons as emergency backup but you're not gonna last long after doomsday with nothing but a pocket full of shurikens.

6.) *Melee Weapons-* Melee weapons are pretty much anything you swing at an adversary with the intention of cutting or bludgeoning them: blades, blunt items, and chains. Everyone should have, and be trained to use, a melee weapon. If you have a rifle that can be fitted with a bayonet, you've got your melee weapon in the form of a short spear. Hold the long gun by the barrel and swing it, you've got a club. Some melee weapons serve duel purposes as tools like a machete, an axe, a staff, or a hammer. Others are "weapons only" such as a chain whip or flail. Melee weapons are essential for the situations when you're too close to use your ranged weapon or you're out of ammunition or if stealth is required. If you plan on relying on melee weapons extensively, you should look into some of the Filipino arts like Arnis and Kali which emphasize weapons training right from the beginning. Many of the more traditional Asian martial arts do not introduce weapons training until the rank of black belt is reached. Weapons training is important! You may think there's not much more to it than swinging a weapon at an opponent but if you don't know what you're doing, you're likely to end up getting your weapon taken away and used against you. If you have not trained you're also as likely to strike yourself as your opponent. Ask most martial artists who have trained with weapons and they can regale you with stories of times they accidentally hit themselves while training.

7.) *Explosives-* Do you have experience using explosives? Have you been trained in using them? Do you know how to make explosives? Do you have access to explosives and/or grenades? If the answer to *any* of these questions is "no", you might want to skip attempting to be a post-Apocalyptic grenadier. Start messing with explosives when you don't know what you're doing and you might not need the Apocalypse to kill or maim you.

8.) *Non-Lethal Weapons-* Non-lethal weapons being any weapons designed to stun or otherwise incapacitate an opponent. Non-lethal weapons include such things such as chemical and pepper sprays, stun guns/batons, tazers, and rubber bullets or beanbag rounds. The humanitarian in you may seek to subdue your opponents with no permanent harm rather than kill or injure them. In some situations this may be admirable and right but it can be dangerous also. Not every hostile may respond to your non-lethal weapon to the same degree. Also, the non-lethal weapon may require you to get closer than desirable to your opponent. You also have to consider how your non-lethal weapon will perform under weather conditions such as high winds or heavy rain. Lastly, how will you acquire refills or batteries for you non-lethal weapons? Like throwing weapons, a non-lethal weapon is not a bad idea to have on your person, however, it should not be relied on as your primary means of defense (unless you meet the qualifications laid out at the beginning of this chapter for a post-Apocalyptic pacifist).

All your weapon choices should ultimately take into consideration these questions:

- Will you be travelling on foot or by vehicle?
- How much time do you have to devote to weapons training?
- What kind of weapons training is available to you?
- Is it just yourself you have to protect or will there be others and if so, what is their level of weapons experience?

Finally, you will have to reconcile your moral and religious beliefs about killing with the need for survival. You can have all the training and weapons in the world but it will do you no good if you don't have the mindset necessary to use them. In the end, the most dangerous man isn't the strongest or best equipped or even most heavily armed, it's the man who has the *will* to kill.

Violence among humans is a complex subject, to say the least, and it would behoove you to spend some extra time studying violent behavior, the roots of human conflict, and non-violent conflict resolution. It will go a long way to helping you understand how you and others will respond to violence.

Chapter 7
THE APOCALYPSE IS MOBILE

The one factor that may make the biggest difference in whether or not you survive the Apocalypse itself, and the days that follow, is mobility.

The Need For Mobility
1.) *Escaping The Apocalypse*- Run for your lives! You may need to physically outrun the events or causes of the Apocalypse such fires, flooding, radiation/toxins, the contaminated, etc.

2.) *Finding Necessities*- The quicker you can move across the terrain, the more likely you are to procure what you need for survival, namely food, water, shelter, medicine, and arms. You may find yourself in a race with other survivors. A race in which the loser may die of thirst or hunger or disease.

3.) *Long-term Trading*- As you adapt to a post-Apocalyptic world, if you want to do more than just survive, you will need to trade with others. Transportation will allow you to hunt and/or scavenge more efficiently and then seek out trading partners.

4.) *Post-Apocalyptic Relocation*- Environmental changes, depletion of resources, epidemics, and invading forces are just some of the reasons why you may find it necessary to permanently relocate your base of operations. A time may also come where settlements may expand to the point that it is advantageous for you to live nearer to one of them.

Do you have the means to stay one step ahead of whatever is bringing down civilization? It's hard to answer that "yes" or "no" simply because you have no idea of what kind of Apocalypse will manifest itself. What you can do, however, is think of the possible Apocalyptic scenarios and then consider what types of transportation will likely be needed especially in relation to where you live. At this point, there are only 3 modes of travel: by land, sea, or air- each having its own variety of possible conveyances.

Land Travel
1.) *Walking-* Walking is how mankind spread across the globe before there was anything remotely resembling what we consider civilization and it may very well be the main mode of transportation once civilization has fallen. Walking has big advantages in that the only fuel needed is food and it's the best way to circumvent obstacles. Walking can be done in any kind of weather and is relatively quiet. The big down sides are that walking is slow and it severely restricts how much you can carry with you.

2.) *Motor Vehicles-* Included here are cars, trucks, vans, golf carts, ATV's, tractors, mopeds, and motorcycles- basically anything with 2 or more wheels and an engine. The big advantage here is speed. Almost any of the above mentioned vehicles will allow you to cover far more ground than you would on foot or even on horseback. The big disadvantage is that they all require fuel in one form or another- gasoline/diesel, ethanol, methane, electricity, hemp seed oil, bio-diesel, or hydrogen. Whichever kind of motor your vehicle has, you will either need to make sure you can secure a regular fuel source or you will need to convert the engine to use a fuel source that is abundant. Ideally, you'd want you or someone you can count on to be capable of providing routine maintenance to your vehicle and maybe even adding some post-Apocalyptic upgrades like armor, weapons, cabin air filters, etc.

3.) *Animals-* Man's first means of rapid transit was on the backs of animals. Horses are the first to come to mind but circumstances may dictate you consider alternatives such as donkeys, oxen, camels, and elephants. The biggest obstacle with mounts is that they have to be trained to be mounts and that training can be difficult and dangerous. You will also have to learn how to care for your mount including what to feed it, how to care for its feet or hooves, how much weight it can carry, etc. The benefits of using a mount is that it can travel faster than you can on foot, it can be used to pull a travois or cart, it can maneuver over terrain most wheeled vehicles would find difficult, and its height can provide you with a better view of the surrounding terrain. One should also not forget the historical advantages mounted cavalry typically had against opponents on foot.

Water Travel

Travel by water has many advantages in that it is less likely you would encounter hostiles and or obstacles. Boats can also make it easier to spot approaching trouble. Ice, however, could restrict your movement in the colder months. Flat-bottomed watercraft would be ideal because they can travel in relatively shallow waters and are easy to beach. There are two basic kinds: powered and unpowered.

1.) *Powered Watercraft-* Powered watercrafts essentially entail the same advantages and disadvantages as motor vehicles except the average person knows even less about boat motors than they do about car engines. Powered watercraft covers all motor-powered craft including regular boats, airboats, personal watercrafts (jet skis/wave runners), hovercraft, houseboats, etc. In a pinch, the average size bass boat can carry a half dozen people plus supplies at about 35-45 mph but it will not afford you much protection from the elements. The average boat motor is also significantly louder than the average car engine and could attract unwanted attention.

2.) *Unpowered Watercraft-* Unpowered refers to any watercraft that is propelled by manual means such as rowing or paddling- rowboats, kayaks, and canoes. Unpowered watercraft may not be as fast or as roomy as their powered brethren but the only energy they require comes from muscle and water currents plus they are one of the most silent means of travel. Furthermore, watercraft such as canoes and kayaks can be carried or dragged across ground with relative ease and, in a pinch, they can be turned upside down to provide a crude shelter from the elements.

3.) *Sailboats-* Sailboats have the advantages of being faster than paddled craft and quieter than powered craft plus many have cabins that allow you to escape from the elements. In the right circumstances, sailboats can be the ideal mode of transport. There are some problems, however. Sailing is a skill and an inexperienced sailor can easily find himself capsized, run aground, or lost at sea. Sail boats are also dependent on wind though many do also sport back-up motors. Another drawback can be the sail boats relatively high profile which can make it visible from some distance away, attracting unwanted attention.

Air Travel

By far, post-Apocalyptic air travel will be the least viable mode of transport. Conditions, such as engine-clogging volcanic ash or hypercanes, resulting from some Apocalyptic events may even make flying next to impossible. Still, every mode of transportation that might carry you away from danger and towards safety should be considered.

1.) *Gliders-* Due to their need to be towed or dropped from a high point, gliders won't be of much use for travel beyond a one-way trip. It doesn't help that they are also not conducive to transporting supplies, equipment, or passengers.

2.) *Dirigibles-* Balloons filled with gases or hot air might provide the most realistic form of post-Apocalyptic air travel in that they don't require much in the way of moving parts and would be easier to improvise repairs on than planes or choppers. You would need to be able to secure the necessary gas or fuel for heat. You will also need to learn to pilot a balloon but that would be a short learning curve compared to trying to learn to pilot a plane. The biggest concern for balloons is that they will be visible for miles away and can be outrun by all other aircraft not to mention balloons are very dependent on good weather. Still they are quiet and don't require a runway to launch or land.

3.) *Airplanes*- Great idea if you are a trained pilot, airplane mechanic, and have a reliable source of aviation fuel plus a runway or know people who are and/or do. Nothing is faster and has the potential to carry so many people and supplies but nothing else makes as many demands either.

4.) *Helicopters*- You need a helicopter pilot and mechanic plus a reliable source of fuel. Still, at least you don't require a runway. Unless you commandeer a military helicopter, you should count on having extremely limited space for passengers and/or cargo.

    Given the number of vehicles that operate on gasoline and diesel, it is quite likely you will be able to use some of them to get around the post-Apocalyptic terrain for some time by scavenging fuel. However, in time those fuels will become more and more scarce. Acquiring some books on producing biodiesel and on converting gas and diesel engines to run on biodiesel might be a worthwhile investment. Some manuals on general auto, motorcycle, and small engine repair would also not be a bad idea to have on hand in case Walmart's Automotive Center is closed after Armageddon.
    The bottom line is you had better put some serious thought into how you're going to negotiate your way through the post-Apocalyptic landscape and have more than one back-up plan. How reliable, fast, protective, and/or stealthy your transportation is may make all the difference in whether you survive the Apocalypse and how well you thrive in the years that follow.

Chapter 8
EAT, DRINK, AND BE WARY

Like so many aspects of the post-Apocalyptic world, your access to food and water will largely be determined by the type of Apocalypse you experience.

In the case of a super-plague, much of humanity may be wiped out but the majority of infrastructure would still be intact meaning, you might be able live off food and water scavenged from stores and homes for years. Assuming animals and farmland were unaffected by plague, you could easily segue into an agrarian or hunter/gatherer subsistence as pre-Apocalypse food runs out or becomes inedible.

Other types of Apocalypses may do just the opposite, they may leave many people still alive but infrastructure and land may be poisoned, irradiated, or otherwise destroyed. In such circumstances, livestock, game much of the pre-Apocalypse preserved food and water may be scarce or non-existent.

What this all means is that when it comes to food and water you need to prepare for the worst and hope for the best.

Water, Water, Everywhere?

The "ancient Mariner" found himself adrift at sea surrounded by water he could not drink. What would happen to the world's freshwater supplies should the polar caps melt and the seas rise, pushing their way up into our freshwater rivers and streams? What if the opposite happened and most of the freshwater became locked up in ice? How about if the freshwater vapor in the atmosphere mingled with sulphur dioxide and then fell back to Earth as acid rain that contaminated ground water? These are just some of the ways an Apocalypse could make water scarce.

The average person is only going to make it three-to-five days without water depending on how active they are, the temperature, the humidity, and what as well as how much, they are eating. Look at any government disaster planning recommendations and a supply of potable water is right at the top of the list. Ask anyone who lives in a hurricane zone how long the bottled water supply in stores lasts when people think there is a hurricane coming. What all this means is that potable water is going to have to be at the forefront of your post-Apocalyptic planning: either getting to it or getting it to you and making sure it is safe to drink.

Most modern Americans take having clean drinking water for granted, even if they live in a desert. Where the water comes from or how it gets to us is seldom considered unless something happens to contaminate the source. For that reason alone, Americans are lucky. There are still many, many parts of the world where access to clean drinking water is a major health issue. Common sources of water-borne illnesses are bacterial, viral, protozoal, and parasitic infections. Here is just a small sample of diseases you can get from drinking infected water:

- Cholera
- Typhoid
- Botulism
- Dysentery
- E. Coli
- SARS
- Dwarf Tapeworms
- Guinea worms
- Legionnaires'
- Hepatitis A

The results of these infections can be, at the mildest, diarrhea and at the worst, slow and agonizing death from a wide assortment of ailments.

Those are just the *usual* water hazards humans face. An Apocalypse could also add to that radioactive contamination from nuclear fallout, acid contamination from volcanic eruptions, and chemical contamination from the breakdown of infrastructure or destruction of industrial facilities.

There are so many things to consider when planning for an Apocalypse, especially when you have no idea what kind of Apocalypse to expect, but securing a source of clean, safe, drinking water has to be at the top of your list no matter what.

What's For Dinner?

The second thing we take for granted in the U.S. is a steady supply of safe food. Despite the occasional instances of E. Coli contamination, America has an incredibly thorough food safety system compared to the rest of the world. How often have you really been afraid to eat something because it might make you sick? Odds are, not too many times. That could quickly change once the Apocalypse arrives.

If you should find yourself fleeing for your lives from hostiles or environmental threats, acquiring enough food to keep you going could be a real challenge. Even if you are an accomplished outdoorsmen, your chances could be slim if flora and fauna have been wiped out or contaminated or there are thousands of other people competing with you for the same sources of nutrition. One would probably be smart to have short-term and long-term food and water plans for both staying put and being on the run.

Even Americans with the poorest eating habits still manage to get a fairly nutritious diet. Nutritional deficiencies in this country are for the most part, a thing of the past. Should obtaining nutrition from a variety of foods become an issue after the Apocalypse, you may find yourself becoming the victim of a variety of nutrition disorders. Here are a few of the possible disorders, which vitamin deficiencies result in them, and what conditions they can result in:

1.) *Rickets-* lack of vitamin D and calcium. Softening of the bones in children. Bone deformation, dental problems, muscle spasms and more.
2.) *Beriberi-* lack of vitamin B1 (Thiamine). Weakness, edema, heart failure, nerve damage
3.) *Pellagra-* lack of vitamin B3 (Niacin). The 4 "D's": dermatitis, diarrhea, dementia, and death.
4.) *Scurvy-* lack of vitamin C. Spongy gums, skin spots, depression, weeping wounds, tooth loss, and death.
5.) *Marasmus-* lack of protein. Wasting away of muscle and other tissue. Can lead to a complete inability to process protein resulting in death.

This is just a taste (no pun intended) of the possible consequences of poor nutrition and doesn't even touch on out-and-out starvation.

In the short run, you may be able to live of the remnants of food preserved before the fall of civilization. While refrigeration will likely break down fairly quickly leaving frozen goods to rot, canned goods may be edible for years to come. But don't expect to be too reliant on canned goods as their shelf-life can be seriously compromised by exposure to temperature extremes as they sit in houses and stores that no longer have functioning air conditioning or heating. In the long run, you *will* have to look to trade, agriculture, fishing, hunting, and gathering for sources of food. If you don't possess any of the skills needed to acquire food in one of those manners, you had better start learning. Once you acquire food, you had also better know how to prepare it and preserve it. Anyone can kill an animal but do you know how to field dress it? Do you know what field dressing is and why it has to be done right? Once the animal is dressed, do you know how to preserve it for 3 days much less for the entire winter? It's a lot to consider but is critical if you want to survive past the shelf-life of canned goods.

Talking About The Taboo

Between 1995 and 1997, tens of thousands of North Koreans starved to death during the famine. Since then, conditions have not much improved. The World Food Programme began to receive reports of human meat being traded at farmers' markets. The North Korean Refugees Assistance Fund interviews of refugees included repeated reports of grave robbing and abductions of children in close proximity to markets. While the paranoid and propaganda-driven North Korean government makes all these claims impossible to substantiate, if the refugees are to be believed, cannibalism is becoming institutionalized in an industrialized nation in the 21st century.

Accusations of cannibalism are often the product of propaganda as one group tries to dehumanize another. But cannibalism during times of famine is a well-documented historical fact. So how likely is the possibility of cannibalism after the Apocalypse? To what extremes will you go to survive? What lines will you cross to save the lives of your loved ones? Most people in America are likely to say *that* is one line they would never cross but then most people in America have never really faced mass starvation. The Apocalypse will shower you with moral dilemmas. What will you eat and under what conditions? Would you want your loved ones to eat you, if it meant keeping them from starvation? What would you do to keep your loved ones out of the hands of would-be cannibals? Ugly questions with ugly answers but ones you had better consider.

Chapter 9
SURVIVOR, HEAL THYSELF

If you've ever been to a Renaissance Fair you may have noticed two Renaissance professions not typically represented- doctor and dentist. Why? Because the reality of medicine and dentistry in those days is so horrific, it would be more appropriate for a haunted house. As much as Americans like to complain about insurance companies, Medicaid, Medicare, VA hospitals, emergency room waiting times, and medical bureaucracy, the truth is modern medicine is truly a blessing.

Those who like to romanticize "the good ol' days" usually neglect to mention things like tooth extractions without anesthesia or the frequency with which women died in childbirth. Just to put it in a little better perspective consider some of these facts:

- According to the Population Reference Bureau, North America has the lowest infant mortality rate in the world (7 infant deaths per 1,000 live births as opposed to Africa's 88 per 1,000)

- The CIA World Fact Book puts the 2008 life expectancy in the U.S.A. at 77.5-80 years old. Compare that to the early 20th century life expectancy of 30-45 years.

- Due to vaccinations, smallpox has been eradicated worldwide. Measles, diphtheria, Hib, and polio cases are at historic lows. There are currently eradication programs underway targeting poliomyelitis and dracunculiasis aka Guinea Tape Worm (World Health Organization).

- A Lancet Oncology study showed that "U.S. survival rates are higher than the average in Europe for 13 of 16 types of cancer".

- The Centers For Disease Control (CDC) cites the fluoridation of American tap water as one of its top 10 health achievements of the 20th century.

In fact, American medicine has advanced so far in its tackling of traditional health threats that the single greatest threat to most Americans is their poor diets and lack of exercise.

Where Did All The Doctors Go?
So when our society and environment all come apart at the seams, how likely is it you'll be able to rely on ambulances, emergency rooms, dentist offices, and the 24-hour pharmacy at Walgreens? What happened to all the paramedics, R.N.s, L.P.N.s, M.D.s, D.O.s, and D.D.S.s? They're still out there somewhere, at least some of them will be, but you're not likely to find them keeping office hours. Oh sure, some will hold out valiantly to the very end but most, like you, will be struggling to keep themselves and their families alive. Some may even conceal their profession for fear of being inundated with patients or fear of being conscripted. Their survival instincts will be just as strong as yours and if faced with choice of saving someone else or saving themselves, they will likely save themselves.

Others may seek to use the value of their professional skills to secure a safe place for themselves with whatever factions hold the most power or resources. It's also possible they are conscripted against their will. Either case may make their services unavailable to you and those in your party. Even if you're able to find the type of medical professional you're in need of, how will you pay for services? It may be a good idea to start cultivating friendships with a few dentists and general medical practitioners now so you might have someone to turn to for help later. You might also want to start considering what services or goods you can trade in exchange for medical help.

Lastly, you might want to map out the locations of all hospitals, emergency care clinics, medical buildings, pharmacies, dental offices, and medical supply stores in your area and on your planned evacuations routes in order to improve the odds that you might find the medical professional you need or at least needed medicines and supplies.

An Ounce Of Pre-Apocalyptic Prevention

Cliché as it may be, an ounce of prevention will definitely be worth a pound of cure after civilization bites the dust. Your healthiness and physical fitness going into the Apocalypse may make all the difference in whether you even survive it and then how well you'll weather the harsh conditions that come next. If you're serious about being ready for the end of the world as we know it then you had better get serious about brushing, flossing, exercise, and healthy eating. You're going to want to do everything you can to see to it that those you hope to have with you after the Apocalypse also start taking better care of their bodies.

There is more to improving your overall health than just diet and exercise. There are other behaviors that jeopardize your health such as recreational drug use, dangerous sports, smoking, brawling, and unprotected sex. These types of behaviors can lead to injuries, conditions, or diseases which will follow you into the post-Apocalypse where they may become more than just nuisances.

To many, this will sound like so much fun will be sucked out of your life you'll be happy see the Apocalypse. The idea is not to make your life miserable but to strike a balance between having fun and preparing your body for the rigors and deprivations to come. Something else to keep in mind is that it may not just be your life that is affected by your level of healthiness in the days of the post-Apocalypse.

If you're not sure where to begin, start by getting a general physical with your regular doctor and then ask him or her for help, resources, and professional references. Also, stop procrastinating and go see your dentist and get done *all* the work that needs to be done. If you think a dentist visit is scary today, just imagine what it'll be like with no meds or electricity.

You should seriously consider starting to take inventory of the medical needs of you and anyone you plan on having with you after the Apocalypse. Does anyone have a chronic condition and if so, how will you cope with that? What about physical handicaps? Some conditions, such as high cholesterol and hypertension may self-correct due to the changes in exercise and diet brought about by the Apocalypse. If there are prescriptions that those in your party must have, you should start compiling information on alternative brands and generic versions of the drugs plus information on their shelf lives.

Finally, as discussed in the previous chapter, start making preparations now so that you have access to clean water and nutritious food so you can avoid medical conditions brought on by contamination and malnutrition.

That Healing Touch

Like so many other areas pertaining to Post-Apocalyptic preparation, you've got a lot to learn. One way to start is by checking with community organizations and local fire departments for free or inexpensive classes on CPR and basic first aid. Your local Red Cross chapter likely also offers classes on pet first aid, standard first aid, and wilderness first aid. Your local government should be able to point you towards Community Emergency Response Team (CERT) Program classes in your area that cover such topics as disaster medical operations. You may even want to go so far as pursuing EMT-B (Basic) certification.

At very least, you should begin building a first aid library so you have somewhere to turn for answers when faced with health problems, injuries, and other medical issues for those times when there are no professionals to be found.

Chapter 10
KNOWLEDGE IS POWER

DO NOT SKIP THIS CHAPTER!

By now you may be feeling over-whelmed by all the things you have to consider, the plans you need to make, the skills you need to learn and that's understandable. But despair not, you can handle it. Consider all the useless junk you house in your memory: sports stats, lyrics to songs you don't even like, directions to locations you plan to never visit again, the names of your grade school teachers. That list just goes on and on and on. If you can learn and memorize so many useless facts, you can learn and memorize what it will take to make it through and beyond the Apocalypse.

Something else to contemplate- you don't have to do it all alone. If your Apocalypse survival plans include members of your family, then you should seriously consider seeking their help in your preparations. They can all be assigned skills to learn or subjects to research. Even if you're talking about including your kids, don't sell them short. Children can be taught to fish, set traps, identify plants, garden, and plenty of other skills. The added advantage of actively including your family is that they the more they learn, the more sense of control they will have over their own destinies. This sense of empowerment, that one is not the pawn of fate, can be crucial to survival. Having plans, having essential skills, reduces the panic one feels when things get crazy. Including your family does something else for you, it gives you a little piece of mind. You'll sleep better at night knowing that your family isn't completely helpless without you; that you've equipped them with the skills needed to survive.

Another option you have is to befriend other likeminded individuals who possess skills and knowledge you do not. Odds are you already have some friends you could start incorporating into your planning. As you work towards acquiring your post-Apocalyptic knowledge, skills, supplies, and equipment you'll inevitably meet others who see the prudence in planning for mega-disasters. Hopefully you'll make trustworthy new acquaintances or even friends with individuals or groups that understand the benefits of combining and sharing knowledge and skill sets.

Recommended Reading

This book has served to open your mind to some of the possible consequences of Apocalyptic-scale events and to suggest some issues and topics you might want to explore further. What follows is a list of recommended books to start you on your way to securing you and your family's future in the event of an Apocalypse. While not comprehensive, this list represents some of the most authoritative books on their respective subjects. There will be some topic overlap in some of these books but you can only benefit from the multiple perspectives. Ultimately it is up to you to determine what subjects you need to study and what kind of library you will need.

By buying this book you have started your journey, now it is crucial to build on that momentum and keep building your knowledge base and reference library. Even if you bought just one book a month, in a year you'll have a library of 12 books and spent approximately somewhere between $120 and $240. It's a good start and a small investment that might just save your life or the lives of your loved ones some day. If you have read this entire book and took the Post-Apocalyptic Survival and Success Assessment (PASSA), then you probably have a pretty good idea of your knowledge gaps and should let that guide you on deciding where to begin building the library that will help you survive and thrive in the face of Apocalyptic events.

The first sentence at the beginning of this chapter urged you not to skip this chapter for a very good reason. It serves to get you thinking about the library you need to build for yourself. As you begin acquiring the books listed below or others like them, do not skip the "recommended reading" section or bibliography. These books will lead you to other books that will help complete the library you need or lead you to even more detailed information on a subject you feel you need to explore further.

Finally, read with a critical mind. You will encounter contradicting information or advice. You will encounter advice that runs contrary to everything you know. When this happens, you need to engage your reasoning skills, challenge your assumptions, and do more research. You'll be glad you did.

FIRST AID

<u>Wilderness Medicine: Beyond First Aid</u>
    Author: William Forgey
    Publisher: Globe Pequot

<u>Ditch Medicine: Advanced Field Procedures For Emergencies</u>
    Author: Hugh Coffee
    Publisher: Paladin Press

<u>Where There Is No Dentist</u>
    Author: Murray Dickson
    Publisher: Hesperian Foundation

<u>Survivalist's Medicine Chest</u>
    Author: Ragnar Benson
    Publisher: Paladin Press

U.S. Army Special Forces Medical Handbook
    Author: Glen K. Craig
    Publisher: Paladin Press

The Hiking Engine: A Hiker's Guide to the Care and Maintenance of Feet and Legs
    Author: Stuart Plotkin
    Publisher: Menasha Ridge Press

DISASTER PREPAREDNESS

Crisis Preparedness Handbook: A Comprehensive Guide to Home Storage and Physical Survival
    Author: Jack A. Spigarelli
    Publisher: Cross-Current Pub.

Making the Best of Basics: Family Preparedness Handbook
    Author: James Talmage Stevens
    Publisher: Gold Leaf Press

Organize for Disaster: Prepare Your Family and Your Home for Any Natural Or Unnatural Disaster
    Author: Judith Kolberg
    Publisher: Squall Press

Self Reliance During Natural Disasters and Civil Unrest: How to Handle Fires, Search and Rescue, and Other Emergency-Response Situations on Your Own
    Author: George R. Bradford
    Publisher: Paladin Press

When All Hell Breaks Loose: Stuff You Need To Survive When Disaster Strikes
>	Author: Cody Lundin
>	Publisher: Gibbs Smith

Wilderness Evasion: A Guide To Hiding Out and Eluding Pursuit in Remote Areas
>	Author: Michael Chesbro
>	Publisher: Paladin Press

It's Time to Plan, Not Panic
>	Author: Barbara Salsbury
>	Publisher: Cedar Fort

Just in Case: How to be Self-Sufficient when the Unexpected Happens
>	Author: Kathy Harrison
>	Publisher: Storey Publishing

FOOD AND WATER

Emergency Food Storage & Survival Handbook: Everything You Need to Know to Keep Your Family Safe in a Crisis
>	Author: Peggy Layton
>	Publisher: Three Rivers Press

Food Security for the Faint of Heart
>	Author: Robin Wheeler
>	Publisher: New Society Publishers

The Ultimate Guide to Small Game and Varmint Hunting: How to Hunt Squirrels, Rabbits, Hares, Woodchucks, Coyotes, Foxes and More
>	Author: H. Lea Lawrence
>	Publisher: The Lyons Press

WILDERNESS SURVIVAL

98.6 Degrees: The Art of Keeping Your Ass Alive
    Author: Cody Lundin
    Publisher: Gibbs Smith

SAS Survival Handbook: How to Survive in the Wild, in Any Climate, on Land or at Sea
    Author: John Lofty Wiseman
    Publisher: Collins

Wilderness Survival: Living Off the Land with the Clothes on Your Back and the Knife on Your Belt
    Author: Mark Elbroch
    Publisher: International Marine/Ragged Mountain Press

Don't Get Eaten: The Dangers of Animals That Charge or Attack
    Author: Dave Smith
    Publisher: Mountaineers Books

URBAN SURVIVAL

Tom Brown's Guide to City and Suburban Survival
    Author: Tom Brown
    Publisher: Berkley Trade

Ragnar's Urban Survival: A Hard-Times Guide to Staying Alive in the City
    Author: Ragnar Benson
    Publisher: Paladin Press

Urban Survival Guide: Learn The Secrets Of Urban Survival To Keep You Alive After Man-Made Disasters, Natural Disasters, and Breakdowns In Civil Order
    Author: David Morris
    Publisher: CreateSpace

DOOMSDAY SURVIVAL

Long-Term Survival In The Coming Dark Age
    Author: James Ballou
    Publisher: Paladin Press

How to Survive the End of the World as We Know It: Tactics, Techniques, and Technologies for Uncertain Times
    Author: James Wesley Rawles
    Publisher: Plume

Life After Doomsday
    Author: Bruce Clayton
    Publisher: Paladin Press

RETREATS

Survival Retreat: A Total Plan For Retreat Defense
    Author: Ragnar Benson
    Publisher: Paladin Press

MARTIAL ARTS

U.S. Marines Close-Quarter Combat Manual
    Author: U.S. Marine Corps
    Publisher: Paladin Press

Arwrology: All-Out Hand-To-Hand Fighting for Commandos, Military, and Civilians
    Author: Gordon E. Perrigard
    Publisher: Paladin Press

Meditations on Violence: A Comparison of Martial Arts Training & Real World Violence
    Author: Rory Miller
    Publisher: YMAA Publication Center

Warrior Mindset
    Author: Dr. Michael Asken, Loren W. Christensen, Lt. Col. Dave Grossman
    Publisher: Human Factor Research Group

MISCELLANEOUS

The Art of Barter: How to Trade for Almost Anything
    Author: Karen Hoiffman, Shera Dalin
    Publisher: Skyhorse Publishing

Auto Upkeep: Basic Car Care, Maintenance, and Repair
    Author: Michael E. Gray, Linda E. Gray
    Publisher: Rolling Hills Publishing

The Eight Essential Steps to Conflict Resolution
    Author: Dudley Weeks
    Publisher: Tarcher

Dangerous Sanctuaries: Refugee Camps, Civil War, And the Dilemmas of Humanitarian Aid
    Author: Sarah Kenyon Lischer
    Publisher: Cornell University Press

How Stuff Works
    Author: Marshall Brain
    Publisher: Chartwell Books

HISTORY

There are far too many great history books to list here but what is important is that you make reading about history a regular part of your Post-Apocalyptic planning. The collapse of previous civilizations and natural disasters has been well documented. Take advantage of that fact to develop your understanding of what to expect when our turn comes. Good subjects to start with include the American South during Reconstruction, the collapse of the Communism in Eastern Europe, and recent events in African states (such as Sudan, Liberia, Somalia, and Rwanda), and anything on natural and man-made disasters. While many of the specific books listed above will not be found in your local library, the same is not true for history books. Your local library is loaded with them and just waiting for you to come and check them out for free! Don't let the opportunity go to waste.

Internet Resources

The great thing about collecting a library of books is that books are not dependent on service providers like electric, cable TV, and phone companies, etc. The books will still be there when the power goes out. The same is not true of the internet. That being said, one would be a fool to not take advantage of the internet in the meantime. The internet abounds with a limitless amount of information that can help you survive in a post-Apocalyptic world. It is also a great way to start networking with like-minded people you can exchange information with or as a way to share your plans and concerns with distant loved ones. So, go on and exploit the internet while it exists but don't be overly reliant on it and back up the information you find there in hard copies that will be available to you long after the internet is dead.

GOVERNMENT

FEMA Emergency Management Institute Independent Study Program
> http://training.fema.gov/IS/crslist.asp

BeReady.gov:
> Disaster and emergency preparedness information and publications
> http://www.ready.gov/

USA.gov Disaster and Emergencies
> Resources For State and Local Employees

NOAAWatch: NOAA's All-Hazard Monitor
> From the National Oceanic and Atmospheric Administration
> http://www.noaawatch.gov

National Institutes of Health
    Disaster Preparation and Recovery
    http://www.nlm.nih.gov/medlineplus/disasterpreparationandrecovery.html

Centers for Disease Control and Prevention
    Emergency Preparedness and Response
    http://emergency.cdc.gov/

United States Access Board
    Resources on Emergency Evacuation and Disaster Preparedness
    http://www.access-board.gov/evac.htm

PREPARDEDNESS AND SURVIVAL

Prepper.org
    Public information site for the Prepper movement
    http://www.prepper.org/

American Preppers Network
    Resources for Preppers
    http://www.americanpreppersnetwork.com/

Survival Topics
    Your Online Survival Kit
    http://www.survivaltopics.com/

Survivalist.info
    Information and resources for survivalists
    http://www.survivalist.info/

Survivalist Boards
    Survivalist forums, gear reviews, and self-sufficiency articles
    http://www.survivalistboards.com

CPSIA information can be obtained at www.ICGtesting.com
Printed in the USA
LVOW080815121112

306925LV00001B/47/P